Day Hikes with Dogs

Western Montana

Wendy Pierce and Becky Warren

PRUETT PUBLISHING COMPANY
BOULDER, COLORADO
pruettpublishing.com

First Edition 2011

ISBN   087108-961-0
      978-0-87108-961-8

Library of Congress Cataloging-in-Publication Data

Pierce, Wendy.
Day hikes with dogs - Western Montana / by Wendy Pierce and Becky Warren.
   p. cm. -- (Day hikes with dogs)
Includes bibliographical references and index.
ISBN 978-0-87108-961-8
1. Hiking with dogs--Montana, Western--Guidebooks. 2. Day hiking--Montana, Western--Guidebooks. 3. Montana, Western--Guidebooks. I. Warren, Becky. II. Title.
SF427.455.P54 2011
796.5109786--dc23

                       2011019431

Cover photograph by James Anderson
Book and cover design by Kay Turnbaugh

For our husbands, Dave and James,
who with good nature and love
put up with our passion for dogs and hiking.

Acknowledgments

We would like to thank and acknowledge those people who provided insight and support for this book. Thanks to Pruett Publishing and Jim Pruett for believing in the concept and making this a reality. Thanks to Kay Turnbaugh, our skilled editor, for her scrutiny, experienced feedback and creative design. Thanks to our friends who are also authors and writers for feedback on the idea, proposal, and navigation through the publishing process. In particular we would like acknowledge Garth Sundem, Christy Stillwell, Jean Arthur, Paul Stein, and Josh Bergan for their assistance and contributions. We would like to thank teachers at a Forest For Every Classroom for their terrific hike suggestions and Wendy's students at Chief Joseph Middle School for their enthusiastic reviews of the hikes. We would also like to thank the many friends who joined us on hikes and graciously provided accommodations during our travels, including Patti Kent, Bob and Liz Keane, and Jim and Christina Grey. Thanks to James Anderson for professional photo shoots with some unprofessional models.

Efforts like this cannot be accomplished without the support of loving families. Sincere thanks to Wendy's family, including Sarah Pierce, Risa Pierce, and her dog-loving mom and dad, Norman and Winnie Elson, who, still in their late 80s, walk their dog every day. Becky would like to thank her entire family, including the Warrens, her mom and dad (Janet and Paul Stein), Douglas Stein, Simon Stein, and Tracy Stein, for their enthusiasm and encouragement.

Finally, it would not be a dog book if we did not call special recognition to our family canines and official trail testers, Milo, Doc, and Uma.

Contents

Introduction

Let's face it—western Montana is dog crazy. On a 10-minute drive across most towns there is a good chance that every car you pass has a furry companion riding shotgun. Rich in beauty and outdoor activity, western Montana is perfect for bringing your four-legged pal along. There are many trails and dog parks in the region, and if you are up for a short drive from most major towns, you can access additional scenic trails ideal for both you and your pet.

We wrote this book from the perspective of avid hikers and dog lovers. There are days we just cannot fit in an all-day hike and love to access some of the trails closer to home. This book is to help you find the right trail for you and your dog, based on your desired locale, distance to walk, and hike difficulty. It provides information and traits about the hike that would be important to a dog hiker, such as plenty of watering holes and horse use (meaning horse droppings, for those dogs that find these great snacks, yet you would prefer them to avoid). Every hike listed is great, that's why we wrote about it, but a few stand out as fabulous and have turned into our favorites. These are marked with 4 Paws Up! These trails have all been tested by our dogs, Milo (Pierce), Doc (Warren), and Uma (Warren) with regular guest appearances from other friends and pets. Milo was not even a year old at the time of this writing, and Doc was 10 years old. To provide variety in dog capability, we have included "their" notes for each hike.

For easy access, there is a matrix that identifies these criteria for hiking. We also have highlighted trails and areas that are specifically leash-required areas. These hikes tend to be in populated or high density wildlife areas and require leashes for at least some of or the entire trail.

We also have included some trails that are wonderful but maybe not the best when taking your dog along, based on the same ranking criteria. Our time outside is precious, so hopefully this will help you narrow down the decision-making process and get you to the trailhead to enjoy your time with your furry friend.

Happy hiking.

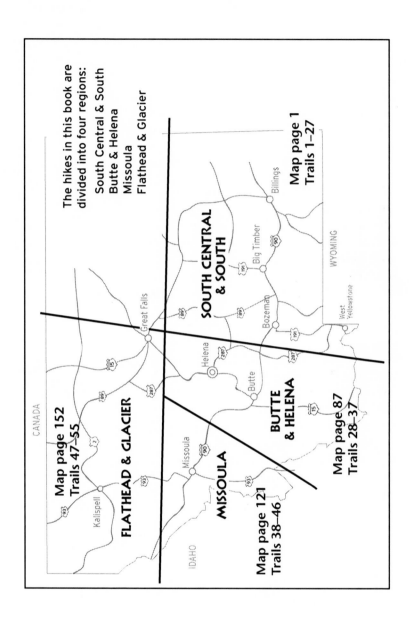

The hikes in this book are divided into four regions:

South Central & South
Butte & Helena
Missoula
Flathead & Glacier

Map page 1
Trails 1–27

SOUTH CENTRAL & SOUTH

Map page 87
Trails 28–37

BUTTE & HELENA

Map page 121
Trails 38–46

MISSOULA

Map page 152
Trails 47–55

FLATHEAD & GLACIER

CANADA

IDAHO

WYOMING

Kalispell
Missoula
Great Falls
Helena
Butte
Bozeman
Big Timber
Billings
West Yellowstone

Hike Matrix

Hike Name	Water	Doggie Difficulty	Hike Distance (Miles)	Horse Poo	Leash Req'd	4 Paws Up!
Bell Lake	P	S	6	L		
Bear Trap Canyon	P	E	1 – 8	N		
Beauty Lake	P	E	4.8	N		
Beehive Basin	S	E – M	4.5	S		x
Blodgett Canyon	P	E	6+	N		x
Blue Lake (Crazies)	P	M	8	S		x
Blue Mountain Rec Area Maclay Flats	S	E	2	N	x	
Bozeman Creek	P	E – M	1 – 12	N		
Bozeman Regional Park	P	E	1 – 2	N		
Crow Creek Falls	P	E – M	6	L		x
Crystal Lake	S	M – S	5.5	N		
Drinking Horse	L	M	3.2	N		
Emerald Lake	P	M	9	L		
Finger Lake	P	E	3	N		
Fourmile Basin Lakes	P	E	8	N		
Garnet Ghost Town	L	E	1	N	x	
Glacier Slough	P	E	2.8	N		
Golden Trout Lake	P	M	5	N		
Hauser Lake	P	E	1.5	N		
Haskill Creek	S	E	4	N		
Hedvig's Trail at Snowfill	L	E	1.2	N		
History Rock	S	E – M	2 – 12	N		
Homestake	S	E	4+	N		
Hugh Rogers WAG Park	L	E	.5	N		
Humbug Spires	S	E – M	6	L		x
Hyalite Lake	P	M	11	S		x
Jacob's Island Bark Park	L	E	.5	N		
Kim Williams Nature Trail	S	E	2.5	N	x*	
Lava Lake	P	M	6	L		
Little Blackfoot	P	E – M	8	L		
Lost Lake	P	E	10	L		x
Lower Cold Lake	P	M	5	N		
MacDonald Pass Continental Divide Trail	N	E – M	7	P		
Middle Cottonwood	P	E – M	4	L		

Hike Matrix

Hike Name	Water	Doggie Difficulty	Hike Distance (Miles)	Horse Poo	Leash Req'd	4 Paws Up!
Morrell Falls	P	E	4.5	N		x
Natural Bridge	S	E – M	.5 – 11	N		
Pattee Canyon	S	E – M	3.4	N		x
Peet's Hill	N	E	2	N		
Pine Creek Falls	P	E	2	L		
Pioneer Falls	P	E – M	4	L		
Point Six Road	N	E	4	N		
Porcupine Creek	P	E	7	L		
Ravine Trail	L	E	6	N		
Rattlesnake Rec Area	P	E – S	1 – 25	N	x*	
Refrigerator Canyon	P	M – S	3 – 16	N		
Rendezvous Trails	N	E	3.7	N		
Sage Creek	S	E	3	P		
South Cottonwood	P	E – M	4	S		
Stanton Lake	S	E	4	L		
Storm Castle	L	M	5	N		
Strawberry Lake	S	M	6	N		
Tahepia Lake	P	M – S	16	S		
Truman Gulch	P	M	4	S		
West Boulder Meadows	P	E – M	6	L		
Windy Pass	S	M	6	L		

Key

Dog and Author Favorite	4 Paws Up!
Water Availability	Plenty, Some, Little, None
Doggie Difficulty	Easy, Moderate, Strenuous
Horse Poo	Plenty, Some, Little, None
x*	Leash required on part of the trail

Dogs on Trails in Montana

General Courtesies

Indeed our trails have many uses. Be aware of bike, horse, and motorized use for trails before you set out. You know the personality of your pets best, and you understand their behavior when around other dogs, horses, and bikers. If they bark at horses or chase bikers, be sure to be courteous and give the riders the right-of-way as you hold your pet.

As much as we love our pets, not everyone is a dog lover. Our dogs happen to be very social and will greet everyone they see, but every now and then we encounter a hiker who cringes when the dogs approach. The message might seem obvious, but if you cannot control your dog by voice command, then best to keep him or her on a leash.

Health and Safety

Most of western Montana is bear country, therefore, most of the hikes in this book are in bear country. Be familiar with bear safety and be "bear aware" before setting out on your hike. If your dogs tend to be roamers and run out of sight, a bear bell is recommended. Not just to warn wildlife of your dog's presence, but to keep you in tune as to where your dog might be exploring.

Typical dog ailments while hiking are dehydration, cuts (usually sticks or barbed wire), or exhaustion. If water sources are limited on the hike, plan ahead and bring an extra water bottle. Cuts can be messy, and if they are not too deep, manageable by the time you are off the trail. Some hikers (or bird hunters) who know that their pets tend to find trouble carry a doggy first aid kit in their vehicle, including staples, topical anesthetic, and bandages. A great reference book is *Field Guide: Dog First Aid Emergency Care for the Hunting, Working, and Outdoor Dog* by Randy Acker and Jim Fergus.

In the spirit of health and safety, a wise Bozeman Emergency Room physician recently said, *"Anyone* can get hurt taking a walk in the woods." As active hikers, we, too, have had some first aid needs in the woods, including rocks to the head. Having a well-stocked first aid kit in your pack or your vehicle can come in very handy, since accidents do happen.

Maps

You should always carry a map of the area you're hiking. The maps in this book are intended only to get you oriented—you shouldn't rely on them to get you to your destination.

Map Key

TH   Trailhead

P   Parking

Ⲁ   Campground

●   Trail destination

---   Trail

=   Road

==   Unimproved road

South Central and South Regions

Doc takes in the Big Sky area views.

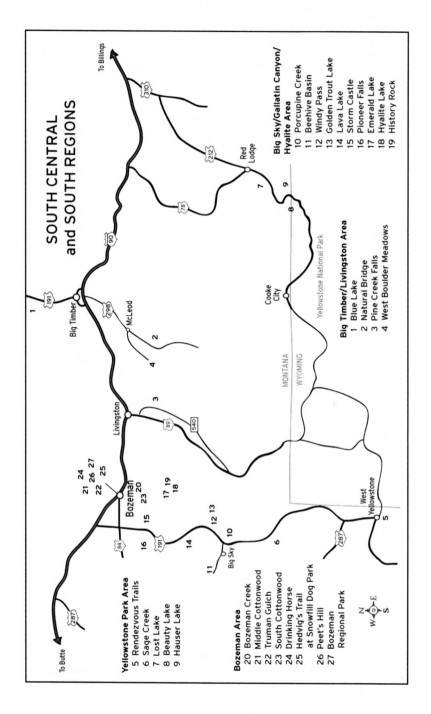

SOUTH CENTRAL and SOUTH REGIONS

Yellowstone Park Area
5 Rendezvous Trails
6 Sage Creek
7 Lost Lake
8 Beauty Lake
9 Hauser Lake

Bozeman Area
20 Bozeman Creek
21 Middle Cottonwood
22 Truman Gulch
23 South Cottonwood
24 Drinking Horse
25 Hedvig's Trail
   at Snowfill Dog Park
26 Peet's Hill
27 Bozeman
   Regional Park

Big Timber/Livingston Area
1 Blue Lake
2 Natural Bridge
3 Pine Creek Falls
4 West Boulder Meadows

Big Sky/Gallatin Canyon/ Hyalite Area
10 Porcupine Creek
11 Beehive Basin
12 Windy Pass
13 Golden Trout Lake
14 Lava Lake
15 Storm Castle
16 Pioneer Falls
17 Emerald Lake
18 Hyalite Lake
19 History Rock

To Billings

To Butte

Big Timber

McLeod

Livingston

Bozeman

Big Sky

West Yellowstone

Red Lodge

Cooke City

Yellowstone National Park

MONTANA

WYOMING

N
W—●—E
S

Milo takes a dip.

Trail #1

Blue Lake (4 Paws Up!)

Distance: 8 miles round-trip
Time: 5–6 hours
Difficulty: Moderate

Overview

One of the best things about writing a hiking book is getting to explore new and amazing areas of the state. Blue Lake, in the Crazy Mountains, is one of the hidden jewels in Montana, and this hike is incredible. It's hard to believe it required writing a book to get to it, and we will definitely return! This hike has it all for both people and dogs.

The trail follows a good size stream that is crossed by several bridges with sun-soaked flat rocks perfect to sit, relax, and throw sticks in the water for your dog. Eventually the trail becomes steeper with a series of switchbacks and heads through rock outcroppings up to Blue Lake and, a little farther along, Granite Lake. For those of you who want to

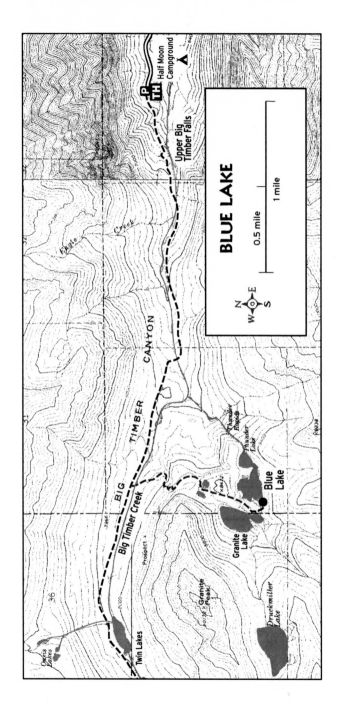

BLUE LAKE

Half Moon Campground

Upper Big Timber Falls

Eagle Creek

BIG TIMBER CANYON

Big Timber Creek

Thunder Rapids

Thunder Lake

Blue Lake

Granite Lake

Druckmiller Lake

Prospect

Granite Peak

Twin Lakes

Oasis Lakes

0.5 mile

1 mile

N
W E
S

do a little fishing, the lake has small rainbow trout, and we saw quite a few rising fish. This is an access point to Crazy Peak and has several backcountry campsites surrounding it. For the day hiker it is great place to rest, have lunch (don't forget to bring something for your dog), and cool off after a fair workout.

Driving Directions

From Bozeman or Livingston take I-90 to Big Timber. From Big Timber follow Highway 191 north for 11.2 miles and turn left (west) on the Big Timber Canyon Road. Follow the road for 1.9 miles and turn right toward Half Moon Campground. You will travel through some gated private property, so make sure to close the gates on your way. The trailhead is on the right just before you enter the campground.

Hiking Directions

From the parking lot, the hike climbs steadily for about 3 miles. Much of the trail (an old Jeep road from mining operations) is wide enough to walk side by and side, so it makes for a nice social outing. The trail follows a stunning stream and has several picturesque bridges. If you are feeling lazy and just want to get out for a short hike or stroll, any of these bridges makes a fine stopping point to toss a ball, sit in the sun, and enjoy the scenery.

There is a short spur trail about a quarter of a mile up the trail to Big Timber Falls, which is definitely worth a detour. After about 3 miles the trail forks to the left, has an unimproved stream crossing (no problem in the fall, but could be tricky in the spring) and climbs steeply through switchbacks to Blue Lake or Granite Lake. If you are enjoying the stream and want a more gradual climb, you can continue straight along the original trail up to Twin Lakes. This is a bit longer (10 miles round trip) and brings you to a wide-open meadow with some incredible views.

Milo's Notes: There was so much to do on this trail, I would have been happy at any of the numerous swimming holes along the way.

Doc's Notes: I really thought they got the name "Crazy Mountains" from watching dogs "go crazy" when hiking. There are several theories

Big Timber Falls is worth the short side trip.

on how the range got its name. One states that the name is short-
ened from Crazy Woman Mountains, after a woman who went mad
and fled to live in the mountains. Another theory is that the range
name was taken from the Crow name, Mad Mountains, for their steep
and rugged grade. I still think it has something to do with dogs—just
watch Milo. He's going nuts.

Milo checks in.

Natural Bridge & Green Mountain Trail 94

Distance:	Varies: a short stroll around the falls area or up to 11 miles round trip on the Green Mountain Trail to Boulder River and back
Time:	½–6 hours
Difficulty:	Easy to moderate

Overview

If you are in the area, Natural Bridge State Park should not be missed. Roaring waterfalls that plunge 100 feet make for spectacular scenery that both you and your dog can appreciate. If you plan to just hike the area around the falls, make sure your dog is either a really good listener or on a leash—we wouldn't want any of them taking a ride down this

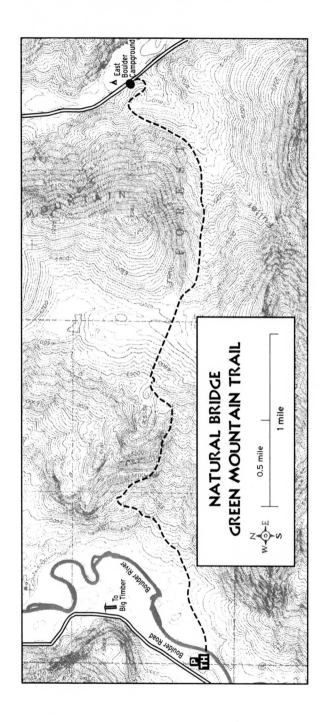

NATURAL BRIDGE
GREEN MOUNTAIN TRAIL

N
W — E
S

0.5 mile
1 mile

East
Boulder
Campground

Boulder River

To
Big Timber

Boulder Road

P
TH

7

river! If you are hiking the Green Mountain Trail, the trail quickly leaves the falls area and becomes safer for your dog.

Driving Directions

From Bozeman or Livingston head east on I-90 and take Exit 397 in Big Timber. Go through the town of Big Timber and make a right going south on McLeod Street, or Highway 298. Continue on Highway 298 for 25 miles through the gorgeous Boulder River Valley, and on the left will be the parking lot for Natural Bridge State Park.

Hiking Directions

From the parking lot there is a paved interpretative trail next to the falls that offers nice views of the Natural Bridge area. (There is actually no natural bridge in the park, it collapsed in 1989.) This is a nice walk, but if you are looking for something more exerting, cross the wooden foot bridge and follow the dirt trail that becomes Green Mountain Trail 94.

This trail has good views of the Natural Bridge area, and after an uphill section it opens up into a meadow with a fantastic panorama of the Boulder River Valley. The trail goes through a thick forest interspersed with meadows. After about 1.5 miles there will be two creek crossings within a mile of each other for a good drink and cool off for your dog. The trail ends at the East Boulder Campground after 5.5 miles, so it is a great one-way hike if you can find someone to shuttle a vehicle, or a long day hike if you want to go out and back.

Milo's Notes: The falls looked like it would be a wild ride, but I am smarter than people think I am. I stayed far away.

Doc's Notes: I am glad there was a vehicle waiting for me at the campground, it was the perfect distance, but out and back would have had me recovering for days.

Pine Creek Falls

Distance: 2 miles round-trip
Time: 30–60 minutes
Difficulty: Easy

Overview

Take you and your doggies to paradise by hiking this popular trail in the Absaroka Mountains, just 10 miles outside Livingston. Along the Yellowstone River Valley, many creeks and veins run into the river, including Pine Creek.

The hike to the falls is an easy one-mile trek that puts you at the creek crossing bridge with a great view of the 100 feet of tumbling waters. If you have more stamina, you can continue on the additional steep 4 miles to Pine Creek Lake. We like this hike because it is so easy to access in the Paradise Valley. Because of that, it is quite popular.

Driving Directions

From Livingston drive south on U.S. Highway 89 for 3 miles to Carter's Bridge, and at Road 540 turn left. The bridge will cross the Yellowstone River, and Road 540 will wind around to continue south on the other side of the river. Continue south for 7 miles to Road 202 and turn left. You will see signs for the Pine Creek Campground. Drive through the campground to the parking area, where the trail-head for Pine Creek and George Lake Trail is well marked.

Hiking Directions

The trail starts off easily with a flat path through the forest. A few hundred yards into your stroll you will encounter the junction for George Lake Trail. (We would recommend avoiding George Lake Trail since it is quite a haul and the trail is not well maintained.) Stay to your left to Pine Creek Falls. The trail climbs gently through the forest, passing ferns and dense growth, and 1 mile in you will encounter the log bridge that crosses the creek and provides central views to the falls. We often take in the views here then jog back for a nice downhill "run."

9

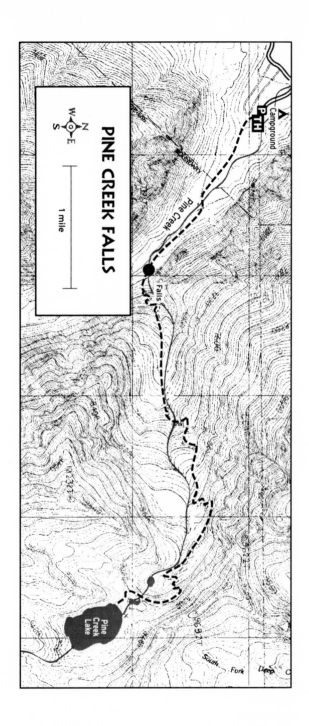

PINE CREEK FALLS

N
W O E
S

1 mile

However, if you want to add more mileage to your trip, you can cross the bridge and switchback for about a half mile to the top of the falls. If this still is not enough for your ticker and your pooch, take the next 3.5-steep-mile climb to Pine Creek Lake. Do not be fooled by a false summit when you come across the first lake. This smaller lake is just below the 30-plus-acre Pine Creek Lake.

Milo's Notes: The shade of the forest is ideal for a fast jog back. Many other dogs to meet and greet during this quick hike to the falls and back.

Doc's Notes: Good length for an 11-year-old sack of Golden bones.

The Pine Creek Falls makes a stunning destination.

The trail to the Meadows.

West Boulder Meadows

Distance: 6 miles round-trip
Time: 2 hours
Difficulty: Easy to moderate

Overview

This hike takes a bit of a drive to get to but is worth it, for it is easy and has a little bit of everything. It is a very well maintained trail, starting in dense forest, leading to a few switchbacks on an open and exposed hillside. It ends in an expansive meadow with great views where the West Boulder River is slow and perfect for doggie paddling. The river is quite popular for anglers, so beware of little Rex jumping into someone's fishing hole.

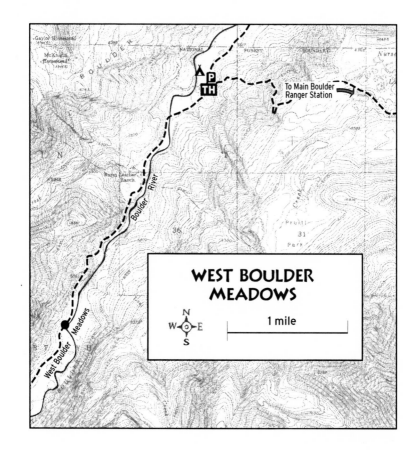

Driving Directions

Take I-90 to Big Timber and exit at Exit 333. Follow the signs to the town of McLeod, heading south for 16 miles. Drive about another half mile just past McLeod to West Boulder Road and turn right, going west. After 7 miles take the first left turn following signs for West Boulder Campground. Drive another 7 miles to the road's end at the trailhead and campground.

Hiking Directions

From the trailhead follow the signs to the trail as it starts about 20 yards on your left. During this first half mile you will have to open an unlocked gate, and the trail continues on the well-maintained path through the thick tree cover. At about 1.5 miles you will come to a large and sturdy bridge to cross the river. There are springs and bogs along the way to this point. The dogs can get to the river for a drink here, but it is a steep scamper to the water at the bridge. After crossing the bridge the trail climbs an exposed hillside switching back a few times, and then it makes an easy traverse for the last mile through new, post-fire growth. During this time you are above the river, and it can be warm late in the day. The trail ends at the meadows with an oasis of slow moving water to enjoy and walk along as long as you desire.

Milo's Notes: This was such an easy hike for me. Once we crossed the bridge heading to the meadows I was on full speed, even uphill, to get to the placid water.

Doc's Notes: I had to be careful going down to the river at the first crossing, as it was steeper than my athletic ability should allow. The flow of the river at the meadows was just my speed, slow.

Doc enjoys the mellow current.

Rendezvous Trails
Rendezvous Loop Trail

Distance: 3 miles round-trip
Time: 2 hours
Difficulty: Easy to moderate

Overview

Although the Rendezvous trail system is mostly known as a cross-country ski area, the trail system welcomes dogs once the snow is gone. Sorry, but no dogs are allowed in the winter—if you want to take your dog skiing in the West Yellowstone area, there is the dog-friendly Boundary ski trail. The Rendezvous system makes a great dog walk before you take your pet into Yellowstone National Park, where dogs are only allowed when on leash and in parking lots or the Old Faithful boardwalk. Being a cross-country ski trail, the Rendezvous trail

15

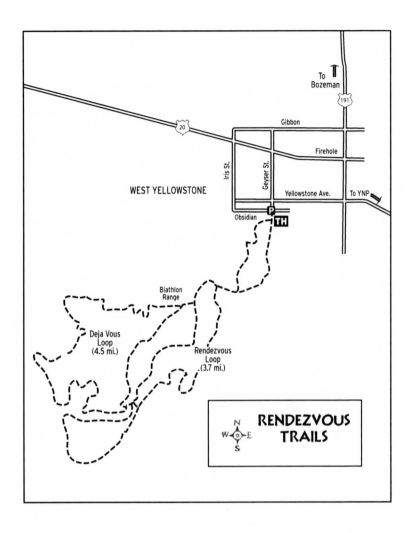

To
Bozeman

191

Gibbon

20

Firehole

Iris St.

Geyser St.

WEST YELLOWSTONE

Yellowstone Ave.

To YNP

P
Obsidian
TH

Biathlon
Range

Deja Vous
Loop
(4.5 mi.)

Rendezvous
Loop
(3.7 mi.)

N
W—E
S

RENDEZVOUS
TRAILS

system weaves a wide path through lodgepole pine forest with a roller-coaster-like variety of ups and downs, however, it never becomes really steep or difficult. There are some nice views along the way and many cutoffs so you can do a variety of paths and still be back in time to get a full day in at Yellowstone. Being in such close proximity to the park, wildlife share these trails, so make sure to bring bear spray and a leash in case some other furry creature is taking a walk with you. If you plan on taking a longer hike, bring water for your dog; there are no water sources in this trail system.

Driving Directions

From Yellowstone Road in the town of West Yellowstone, head south at the stop light (going north will take you to Yellowstone National Park). Travel less than a half mile to a parking lot on the left for the trailhead. This is an easy walk from town as well.

Hiking Directions

From the parking lot and the warming hut/restrooms go straight on the trail for about a half mile. At this point you will cross a Forest Service road and enter the main trail system. Head up a short hill, and there is a map and sign that show all the area options. To the left is the Rendezvous Trail. This is 3.7 miles long with some ups and downs to Cabin Hill, which is the halfway mark. From there it heads back to the Biathlon Range. At the Biathlon Range take a right, and that will take you back to the entrance. There are plenty of cutoffs that have well marked trail maps, so if you want to turn back early there are a lot of options.

Milo's Notes: I have spent a lot of time in the car waiting for skiers; this time I got to explore the trails and see what all the fun is about.

Doc's Notes: This is just perfect before a day in Yellowstone. I get to stretch my legs and run around a bit, so I am ready to hang out in the car and watch the scenery.

The view along Sage Creek Trail.

Trail #6

Sage Creek

Distance: 3 miles or longer round-trip
Time: 2 hours
Difficulty: Easy

Overview

Sage Creek is a good and easily accessible hike in the Yellowstone Park area. It can be a short, pre-Yellowstone Park hike so your dog can get in some leg-stretching before a day in the car, or a longer hike in the Gallatin Canyon. The hike is generally flat and follows a scenic jack fence line that goes through a mixed forest of lodgepole pine, aspen, and sage brush. There are some nice views all along the trail. We recommend this hike for a cool fall day, since there is not much water for the first mile and a half. The colorful aspen groves make a perfect hike for September or early October. As always in the Yellowstone area, be bear aware, since this area is home to grizzly and black bears.

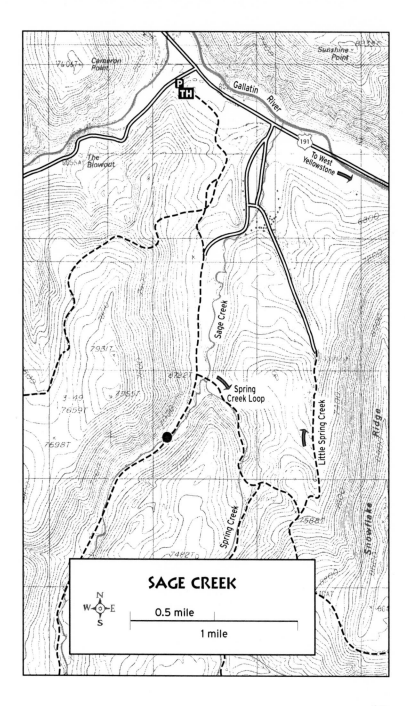

Cameron
Point

76067

Sunshine
Point

Gallatin   River

P
TH

191

To West
Yellowstone

The
Blowout

0058A

Sage Creek

7931T

8722T

Spring
Creek Loop

79657

79557

76597

Little Spring Creek

Snowflake   Ridge

76987

Spring   Creek

15887

7482T

SAGE CREEK

N
W   E
S

0.5 mile

1 mile

Driving Directions

Follow Route 191 through Gallatin Canyon. The Sage Creek trailhead is 13.7 miles south of the Big Sky turn on the right (west) side of the canyon. If you are coming from West Yellowstone, the trail is 33 miles north on 191, on the left (west) side of the canyon.

Hiking Directions

From the parking lot the trail starts with a slight uphill through a mature open forest. Stock parties frequently use the trail, so there are several parallel trails, any of them can be followed, but we stayed on the lowest one closest to the fence. There are several gates to go through and after three-quarters of a mile there is a trail junction. Stay on the Sage Creek Trail, and in about five minutes there is a large gate and several trails going down the hill. If your dog is really thirsty, take a quick detour down the hill to a slow-moving creek for a cool-off and a drink. There is also a nice view of the Elkhorn Ranch cabins, but make sure to stay on the public access. The trail continues, and it is another 20 minutes until you hit your first water source. From there go through the gate, and the trail has good access to the creek. We found this was a good turnaround for a short hike.

For a longer hike, the trail connects with Spring Creek and brings you back in a loop to Highway 191 along Little Big Spring Creek, following the arrows on the map.

Milo's Notes: I got a little thirsty on the trail, but my tongue never got to my knees. It was easy, flat, and the sage had good smells.

Doc's Notes: I was glad to head down the hill for a drink—a little too long without water—but once I was refreshed, the length and slope were just perfect.

Lost Lake (4 Paws Up!)

Distance: 10 miles round-trip
Time: 5 hours
Difficulty: Easy

Overview

This is a beautiful hike along a roaring creek with multiple pools and sloughs along the way. At the gateway to the Beartooth Mountains, this trail is easily accessed just outside Red Lodge. It is a straightforward trail with plenty of scenery, ending at a tranquil mountain lake. What's not to like?

Driving Directions

From Red Lodge, drive south 8.5 miles on the Beartooth Highway (Route 212) to the Lake Fork turnoff on the west side of the road. Take this 2 miles to the trailhead.

Hiking Directions

From the trailhead, take the path that crosses the creek on a well-established bridge. This is the only creek crossing. You will follow the trail to the right along the creek on an easy and pleasant uphill. The path varies from being wide and smooth to parts that are rockier. Along the way you will see colorful pools in the creek that are great for doggie drinking opportunities.

After about 3 miles, the trail opens up, and there is a meadow to the right where the creek has slowed to a slough called Broadwater Lake. This is a great snack and swim stop before going the last 2 miles to Lost Lake. From Broadwater Lake you lose sight of the creek and continue up the path through the forest for about 1.5 miles to where a trail sign directs you to the left to Lost Lake. The last half-mile takes you up through a wooded area, landing at the placid and spacious lake.

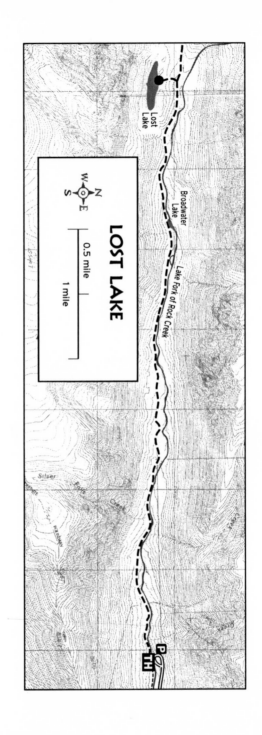

LOST LAKE

N
W · E
S

0.5 mile
1 mile

Lost Lake

Broadwater Lake

Lake Fork of Rock Creek

Silver

P TH

Milo checks out the forest from the shores of Lost Lake.

Milo's Notes: So many swimming holes, so little time.

Doc's Notes: Ten miles for this old dog? It was no problem with a pleasant grade the entire time and plenty of opportunities to cool off.

Crane Lake on the way to Beauty Lake.

Beauty Lake/Beartooth Plateau

Distance: 2.4 miles one way to the lake,
but longer loops are possible
Time: 3 hours
Difficulty: Easy

Overview

Although most of the Beartooth Plateau is officially in Wyoming, residents of Montana tend to claim it as part of our own state. If you are in the Yellowstone Park area, a side trip to the Beartooth Plateau is a must.

Dog regulations are the same here as in any National Forest, so leashes are not required. The hiking is generally easy without much elevation gain, since most of the elevation gain is reached by driving up Beartooth Pass. Hikes in this area allow access to incredible scenery and alpine lakes more quickly than most other hiking areas.

With that being said, Beauty Lake sits at an elevation of 10,064 feet, which means that those of you who live at lesser elevations (which is most of us) might feel the thin air at that elevation in your lungs, even when the hiking is easy.

The plateau also is known for having many mosquitoes, since it keeps snow so long. However, if you are prepared with repellent or go in the fall, this hike makes for an incredible day.

Driving Directions

This hike can be accessed either from Red Lodge or Cooke City. From Red Lodge, follow the Beartooth Scenic Highway (Route 212) 39 miles to the Beartooth Lake Campground, which will be on your right. From Cooke City, drive east for 23 miles, and the campground is on the left side of the road. Once on the campground road, follow signs past the boat launch and into the campground. Keep going until you see a sign for the trailhead (just past the last loop). There is a small parking area next to a stream.

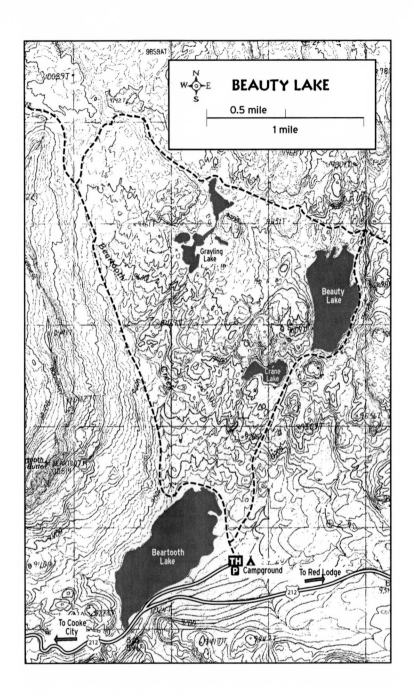

BEAUTY LAKE

0.5 mile

1 mile

Grayling
Lake

Beauty
Lake

Crane
Lake

Beartooth
Lake

TH
P Campground

To Red Lodge

To Cooke
City

212

Hiking Directions

The trail was a little difficult to find, and we ended up walking too far and having to turn back. There is a path from the parking lot that heads toward Beartooth Lake. Follow that, but as soon as you cross the first stream, look for a somewhat primitive trail to the right, which very quickly becomes a much more well-traveled path up into the surrounding forest.

The hike goes uphill pretty steadily for at least a half hour through a mixed forest, primarily consisting of white bark pine, a high elevation species. After the trail levels out it is just a short walk to the small, but stunning Crane Lake. Take some time to walk down to the lake for a swim for the dogs—or really brave humans—or for some well-deserved rest.

Beauty Lake is much larger and not far beyond Crane Lake. The trail follows the east side of the lake, and from there you can either turn back to the parking lot, make a loop following trail 619, or travel off trail to many of the other lakes in the area.

Milo's Notes: It was so good to get out of the car after traveling through Yellowstone Park. I just don't understand why I couldn't go wander with those other really big dogs that Wendy kept calling bison.

Dave and Milo walk the trail to Hauser Lake.

Hauser Lake/Beartooth Plateau

Distance: 1.5 miles or longer
Time: 1 hour
Difficulty: Easy

Overview

If you are looking for a really short but scenic hike in the Beartooths, Hauser Lake has some wonderful views, a lake for a swim, and is quick enough to stretch your and your dog's legs before or after a day of sightseeing in Yellowstone National Park.

Driving Directions

This hike can be accessed either from Red Lodge or Cooke City. From Red Lodge follow the Beartooth Scenic Highway (Route 212) 27.3 miles to a small pullout on the right-hand side of the highway. From Cooke City, drive east on Route 212 for 34.2 miles and the pullout is on the left side of the road. The trail is on the opposite side of the road, so make sure to watch your dog as you cross the highway to get to the trail.

Hiking Directions

Across from the pullout there is a well-marked sign and mileage for that part of the Beartooth Recreation Loop. Hauser Lake is a short walk that is slightly downhill with beautiful views of the surrounding mountain ranges and lakes. Once at the lake, you can either turn around or continue along Trail 614 to several other lakes.

Milo's Notes: OK, this was so short I barely got going, and it ended. The big wide spaces were great to run around and get a little more exercise in before more car time.

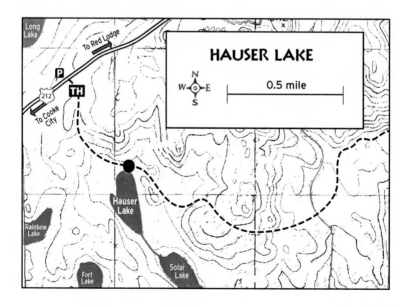

Milo, Doc, Uma, and Becky all enjoy a creekside break.

Trail #10

Porcupine Creek

Distance: 7 miles round-trip
Time: 3 hours
Difficulty: Easy

Overview

It is hard not to enjoy a hike that provides commanding views of mountain peaks, but especially Lone Peak at Big Sky. This trail is easy to access, as it is just past the Big Sky turnoff and is an easy but diverse landscape for you and the pup's pleasure. The trail is also popular with mountain bikers and has its share of horse traffic. However, most bikers stick to the trail and don't cross the creek at mile one.

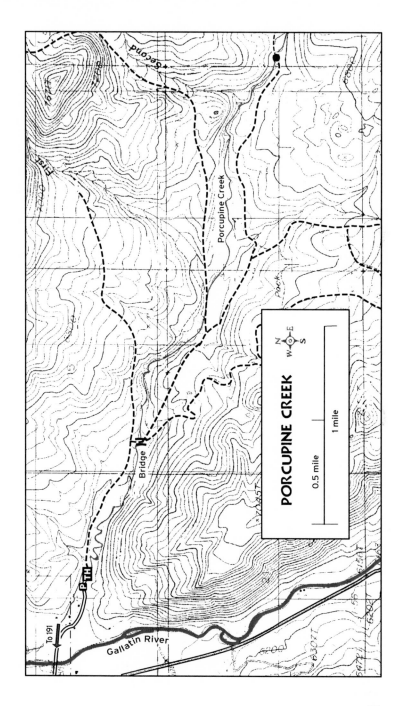

31

Driving Directions

Take U.S. Highway 191 2.5 miles south of the Big Sky turnoff (Big Sky Road). The road is marked with signs for Porcupine Creek. Take this one-half mile to the trailhead parking area.

Hiking Directions

The trailhead is well marked and is a wide, Jeep-like path for the first mile. The creek will be on the right until you cross the bridge. The trail provides views to the open valley and hillsides to the south. After a mile, the trail splits; follow it to the right, taking the bridge across the river. You will see a sign for Ramshorn Lake and Windy Pass. Take the trail to the left up a slight hill. The trail continues to roll with the creek on your left. At the next mile, there is another sign for Ramshorn Lake. Follow this trail to the left where it rolls again through valleys sprinkled with aspen groves. The last half mile will take you to the creek again. This is a good place to take a break, let the doggies have a dip, and follow your path back.

If you want to continue farther, there is no easy creek crossing here, so it is best to have a pair of water shoes handy if you want to explore more. The return trip lets you enjoy the view of Lone Peak for most of the journey.

Milo's Notes: This hike let me roam free for hours with plenty of water stops on the way. I did have my moments with all-you-can-eat horse dropping snacks. Probably more than I should have.

Doc's Notes: This was another great distance and terrain for this active senior. No scrambles or climbs.

Uma's Notes: Oh, did I get "birdy." Great habitat for grouse. I hope to come back this fall.

Beehive Basin and its lakes.

Beehive Basin (4 Paws Up!)

Distance: 4.5 miles out and back
Time: 3 hours
Difficulty: Easy to moderate

Overview

Beehive Basin is one of the premier hikes in the Big Sky area. This high alpine bowl is nestled among the 10,000-foot peaks of the Spanish Peaks in the Lee Metcalf Wilderness Area. The hike takes you through incredible fields of wildflowers and alpine meadows and terminates in a glacial valley with a small lake, perfect for a swim and a game of catch with your dog. But make sure to give any anglers space! There is ample water along the way and plenty of room for your dogs to run and sniff to their heart's delight. Although this is a popular trail,

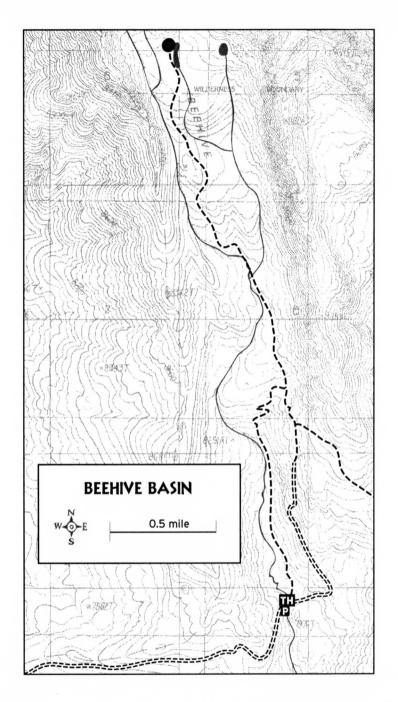

BEEHIVE BASIN

0.5 mile

Wendy flanked by Tank and Milo.

it is very dog friendly. Several of the people we passed were dog owners here on vacation. They were happy to give our dogs a good pet as we passed and traded stories about their dog friends that they left at home.

A nice way to end the day is to take a short trip over to Moonlight Basin, sit on the deck, have a cold beverage, and watch the world go by on a summer's day.

Driving Directions

From Bozeman, drive south on Highway 191 to the turnoff for Big Sky and turn right. Drive the Big Sky Spur Road approximately 9 to 10 miles, until it turns to gravel. If you are coming from Big Sky, turn west toward Moonlight Basin. Turn right at Beehive Basin Road just before the Moonlight Basin gate. Follow this road approximately 2.5 miles, winding through private developments, and whenever the road turns right, turn right. The trailhead is at the bottom of a steep hill. The parking lot is very small and fills up quickly, so if you get there late, be prepared to walk a bit to the trailhead.

Hiking Directions

The hike starts by crossing a bridge and heading up switchbacks through a meadow. A few Big Sky "vacation" homes are along the trail, but you will lose these soon and have the feeling of really being in the high backcountry. The trail meanders through meadows filled with wildflowers. This is moose country, and there are often reports of sightings in the meadows.

The trail follows a stream pretty much the whole way for your dog. There are several stream crossings, and you also will go through a marshy area, so be prepared to have wet feet.

Just before the first of the two lakes toward the end, the trail gets steeper and might have you breathing hard in this thin air, but don't worry, it doesn't last long. After the first lake, the terrain evens out to the final lake, surrounded by glacial boulders that make a perfect spot to sit, throw a ball, and have a bite to eat (make sure to bring a snack for your dog as well).

Milo's Notes: We did this hike in mid-July, and it still had enough snow for me to roll around in!

Tank's Notes: I was visiting Milo when we did this—I jumped on him the entire way.

Doc's Notes: I am pretty sure I heard Becky and Wendy come up with the idea to write this book while we were hiking here. It worked out well for me—it means more hiking, which I love to do! I also got a whole lot of pets (and a treat or two) from vacationers missing their dogs. This wasn't too hard on my aging hips.

View from Windy Pass.

Windy Pass

Distance: 6 miles round-trip
Time: 3 hours
Difficulty: Moderate

Overview

This hike leads to commanding views of the Gallatin, Madison, and Absorka Ranges, with plenty of watering holes on the way. The bumpy road keeps this trail a little less traveled than others in the Gallatin Canyon. The diverse landscape through forest and subalpine terrain is full of wildflowers for both furry and non-furry walkers to enjoy.

Driving Directions

From Bozeman, head to Four Corners on Huffine Lane. At Four Corners turn left (south) on Highway 191 for 30 miles to Portal Creek Road, #984. Turn left (east) on Portal Creek Road and take it about 6 miles to the trailhead. The road is bumpy and rocky, so it is slow going. It will take about 20 to 30 minutes to drive the 6 miles to the trailhead.

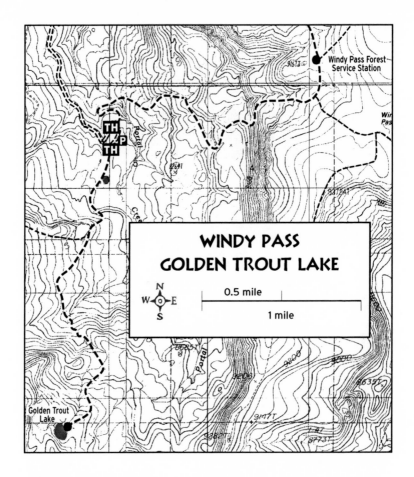

Hiking Directions

Take the Upper Portal Creek Trail to the left of the trail sign and bulletin board. You will have a creek crossing early in the hike, which can be done by hopping rocks or balancing over some gathered logs. This first creek crossing can be very high in the spring with runoff. From here the trail climbs, switchbacking through conifer forest covered in old man's beard and boulder fields. There are a few more creek crossings and springs, providing some muddy holes for a quick drink for your dog before you clear the trees.

At 2.5 miles the trail brings you to an open meadow surrounded by lush hillsides and a view of the Forest Service cabin on your left. Follow the trail to the left heading toward the cabin. If you are interested in spending a night or two, the Forest Service website says the cabin is available for rental. There is a well-maintained outhouse about 20 yards left of the cabin. From here you can take the trail behind the cabin up about a half mile to the vista. At the top you can see three surrounding ranges, the Madisons, Gallatins, and Absorkas. Look to the west, and you can see the distinctive diamond face of Lone Peak. The hills between the cabin and the pass provide a jolly playground for running pups, plus the Windy Peak breeze provides some well-deserved relief from the climb.

Milo's Notes: I loved being able to tear around in the meadows at full speed, so much to sniff, so little time.

Doc's Notes: I found this to be just enough climb and distance for my old bones. I really liked the shade of the cabin while we took a snack break.

Becky, Doc, Uma, and Milo take a break by the Windy Pass Forest Service cabin.

Golden Trout Lake.

Golden Trout Lake

Distance: 5 miles round-trip
Time: 4 hours
Difficulty: Moderate

Overview

A lovely lake filled with feeding trout awaits you at the top of this trail. The mileage is short to the lake, and the climb is steady and a bit exerting, though not strenuous. There is plenty of water on the way for hot and thirsty hounds.

Driving Directions

The directions are the same for Windy Pass, hike # 12. From Bozeman, head to Four Corners on Huffine Lane. At Four Corners turn left (south) on Highway 191 for 30 miles to Portal Creek Road, #984. Turn left on Portal Creek Road and take it about 6 miles to the trailhead. The road is bumpy and rocky, so it is slow going. It will take about 20 to 30 minutes to drive the 6 miles to the trailhead.

Hiking Directions (see map on page 38)

There are two trailheads at the parking area, Golden Trout Lake and Windy Pass. The trail for Golden Trout is at the far end of the parking area, to the right of the trail postings board.

The trail starts through lodgepole pine forest, and there are a couple of small ponds within the first quarter mile (which is a nice final cool-off spot for the return trip).

At 0.5-mile is a trail junction marking trails for Golden Trout Lake and Hidden Lakes Trail. At this junction, stay left. A mile into the hike you will come to the first creek crossing. There are rocks to hop across, but you might have to look around for the best place to cross. From here the trail is a steady uphill climb all the way to the lake with a few springs along the way for the dogs to lap. Head to the far end of the lake, which is bordered by a boulder field providing plenty of seating spots where you can enjoy your destination.

Milo's Notes: This was a true doggie fitness course. I loved the final pond swim just before reaching the car.

Doc's Notes: I was a little tired after the final push up, and I had to limit my swimming to just a few stick fetches. The water was great, and there were easy banks to jump from.

41

Lava Lake.

Lava Lake

Distance: 6 miles round-trip
Time: 3–4 hours
Difficulty: Moderate

Overview

We love hiking to lakes, and Lava Lake is no exception. However, MANY hikers and dogs like this trail as well, because it is so accessible. It is an easy trailhead to find in the Gallatin Canyon with a great destination. If you can get to the trailhead early, before 9 a.m., you will be hiking in solitude and likely only see people and other dogs during your descent. The lake is expansive with rocky outcroppings. You can climb up a cliff and watch your dogs swim as you supervise over snacks. It is a steady and gradual elevation gain of about 1,600 feet to the lakes and is manageable for people and puppies in decent shape.

Driving Directions

From Bozeman drive west on Main Street as it turns into Huffine Lane, to the town of Four Corners, and turn left. Take Highway 191 to the Lava Lake Trail exit between mile markers 65 and 66. The turn is just before the 35 MPH bridge (named for the 'Slow to 35mph' sign). If you are driving from Big Sky, you will have to pass the bridge and entrance and go to a marked turnaround and then backtrack.

Hiking Directions

The trailhead is well marked, and the trail has a steady and manageable climb the entire time. The rocky trail passes through lodgepole pines for the first mile. Shortly after that, there is a foot bridge, and this is the only creek crossing you will encounter. It is a good watering hole for the hounds. Continue up the switchbacks for the final climb to the lake, where the view opens up dramatically. The foot of the lake is inviting for dogs to take a swim. The lake has plenty of rocky seating in the area for you to soak in the view and enjoy a snack. If

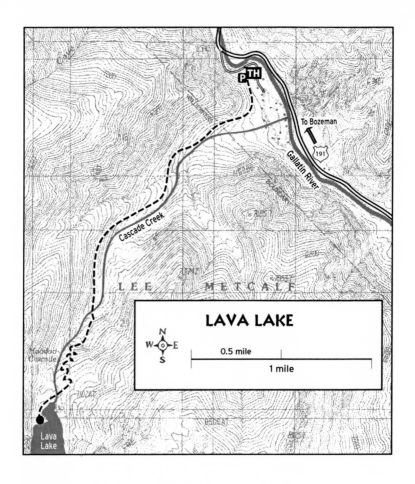

you desire to explore, the official trail ends here, but you can trace the well-traveled steps of others around the lake.

Milo's Notes: The rocks by the lake were not very flat, therefore, a few snacks went rolling away—I smelled opportunity and managed to get a few extra morsels—I must admit, that Doc is pretty fast when it comes to food! This is like a playground. On the way back, we saw many more dogs to play with.

Doc's Notes: Liked the not-so flat-rocks!! Please bring more sticks.

View along Storm Castle Trail.

Storm Castle

Distance: 5 miles round-trip
Time: 3 hours
Difficulty: Moderate

Overview

One of the first hikes to lose its snow in the springtime, Storm Castle is a popular destination in the Gallatin Canyon for many hikers and dog walkers. The trail switchbacks with gradual to moderate inclines for most of the way, until you reach the ridge where it follows a wooded path that leads to a natural rock arch. Although there is no water along the way, the hike is short enough and shady enough in

45

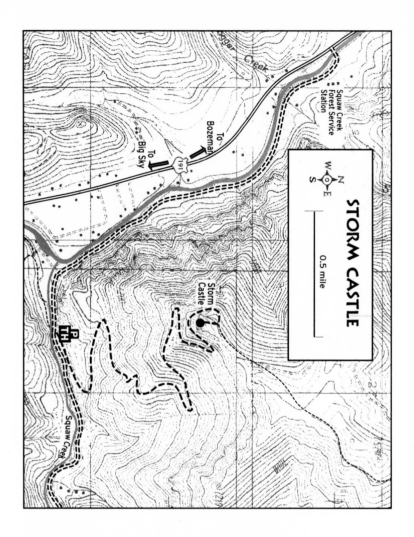

spots that it works as long as you carry some extra water for the dogs. It is also common for there to still be patches of snow along the way, which gives the dogs a great cooling-off spot! Beautiful views, early flowers, and other dogs make this a really nice hike, but be cautious of hot summertime temperatures. The hike is known for ticks, so do a tick check for both you and your dog when you finish. There is a great stream across from the parking lot to let your dogs cool off and get a good drink at the end of the hike.

Driving Directions

This hike is 26 miles south of Bozeman. From Bozeman take U.S. Highway 191 south for 23 miles to the Storm Castle turnoff (5.5 miles once you cross the bridge going into the canyon). Turn left (east) and travel 3 miles to the parking area. From Big Sky, travel north approximately 19 miles until you see the sign for the Storm Castle on your right.

Hiking Directions

The trailhead is on the east side of the parking lot. It immediately starts to climb through a mixed open forest of ponderosa pine and juniper. After about a mile of steady switchbacks and climbing, there is a nice side trail to a limestone cliff with great views of the Gallatin Range. It's a perfect place to stop and give you and your dogs a drink. After that, look for snowfields to cool off in as the trail continues to climb through loose talus slopes and up to the ridge. There are great views along the way, and the trail is well-used and nicely maintained.

Uma's Notes: I got in trouble on the trail. There were birds to flush, and I couldn't resist. Silly people forgot to bring a leash, and I ended up having to be tied with a pair of rain pants—how humiliating. I hope no other dogs saw me.

Doc and Milo's Notes: We had to wait a long time for Uma, good thing there were lots of other dogs and dog owners to talk to on the trail and to see if they had seen Uma—thanks to the people who found her and brought her back!

The view of Spanish Peaks from the trail.

Trail #16

Pioneer Falls

Distance: 4 miles round-trip
Time: 2–3 hours
Difficulty: Easy to moderate

Overview

Stunning mountain views, wildflowers galore, and a waterfall destination make Pioneer Falls a terrific day hike with your hounds. The hike does have a good amount of horse traffic, complete with droppings, so if your pup likes to snack on such apples, be prepared. Also, there is about a 30-minute span where you switchback toward the falls and away from water. There always seems to be a water source just when the dog panting gets heavy, but just in case it ends up being a hot day, we like to bring an extra bottle.

Driving Directions

From Bozeman drive west on Main Street as it turns in to Huffine Lane, to the town of Four Corners, and turn left. Take Highway 191

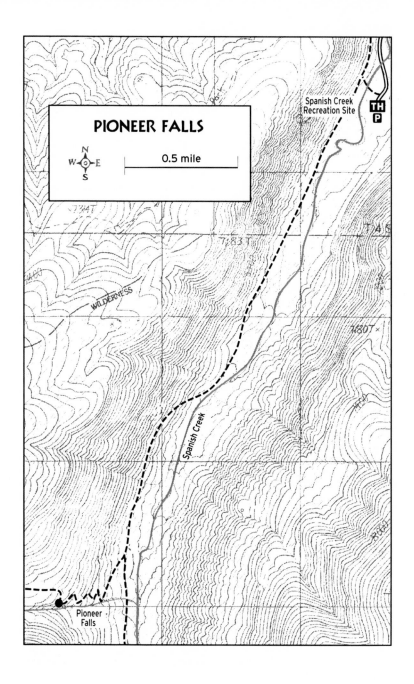

PIONEER FALLS

N W E S

0.5 mile

Spanish Creek
Recreation Site

Spanish Creek

WILDERNESS

Pioneer
Falls

south about 13 miles to Spanish Creek road and turn right (west). Take this about 9 miles (past Ted Turner's gorgeous Flying D Ranch) to the wide parking lot at the Spanish Creek campground.

Hiking Directions

Take the wide bridge across the creek and go left, following the South Fork of Spanish Creek. You will lose sight of the creek after the first half mile, so make sure the mutts take a pre-hike swim. The hike follows the creek and is relatively flat through tree cover. After about a half hour, the trail will open up to a meadow and veer to the right. There is a sign directing hikers to the falls about another mile ahead. From the meadow, the trail begins a climb, switching back and forth to the falls. The views of Beacon Point, Gallatin Peak, and Blaze Mountain are gorgeous, and you are sure to spot a variety of wildflowers.

You will be led back into some shade in the forest before the last short switching climb to the falls. It is a good place to have a swig of water to stay hydrated, enjoy the rumble of the 30-plus-foot falls, and then make your way back down. There is a small pool that the dogs can wade in, which is out of the current, but keep your eyes on them, so they don't take an unexpected leap over the falls.

Doc's Notes: I like to wade above the falls and take it all in. A perfect spa before heading back down.

Uma's Notes: I love the uphill switchbacks. They really test my stamina.

Doc peers into the falls.

View of Emerald Lake.

Trail #17

Emerald Lake

Distance: 9 miles round-trip
Time: 5 hours
Difficulty: Moderate

Overview

The Hyalite area abounds with lakes, waterfalls, and creeks. It attracts recreationists year round, because of its proximity to Bozeman. Its popularity is definitely noticeable during the weekends, so if it is possible to hike during the week, you will be guaranteed more solitude. It takes about 45 minutes to get to the trailhead for Emerald Lake from town. Although it is a longer trail with a moderate climb, it is fine for anyone with good fitness and time. The hike offers the final reward of a stoic alpine lake, perfect for a lunch spot, stick fetch, and even a wade in the water for the people in your party on a hot day. Since the

51

hike is a 9-mile round-trip, plan accordingly to avoid being up high during afternoon thunderstorms.

Driving Directions

From Bozeman drive to Hyalite Canyon Recreation area by taking 19th Avenue south. At the sign for Hyalite Canyon, take a left (east) on Hyalite Canyon road, and travel about 11.5 miles to the reservoir. The road crosses the dam and follows the reservoir. After getting to the head of the lake, the road crosses the East Fork of Hyalite Creek, and there is a fork in road. Take the left fork, which continues as a dirt road for about 2 miles to the trailhead.

Hiking Directions

The first few miles of the trail switchbacks through timber and can be damp in the early season. The shade gives way after about 2 miles and opens to views of the surrounding mountains. The trail follows the East Fork of Hyalite Creek, and, though it is not always at your side, it is reachable by four paws for mid-hike drinking. The last mile to the lake you will find yourself surrounded by peaks in a stunning basin. Emerald Lake is a good sized alpine oasis at roughly 9,000 feet. Find a place to sit, enjoy its clarity, and serve a Milk Bone. If you still have some energy and want to keep going, you can continue on the trail for about a half mile to Heather Lake. Otherwise, to descend, simply follow the trail back the way you came.

Milo's Notes: If we go on Saturdays, I am sure to find a mountain biker to keep pace with.

Doc's Notes: This is a long one. About as far as I should go at my age, but the climb isn't too rough, and the lake is certainly therapeutic. I might leave this one to the puppies.

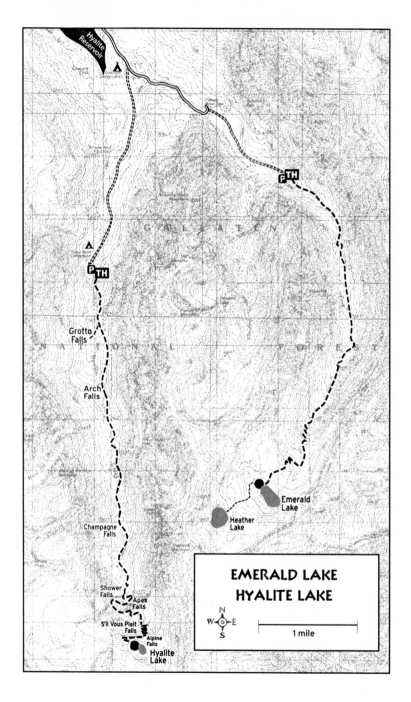

EMERALD LAKE
HYALITE LAKE

1 mile

Hyalite
Reservoir

P TH

P TH

Grotto
Falls

Arch
Falls

Champagne
Falls

Shower
Falls
Apex
Falls
S'il Vous Plait
Falls
Alpine
Falls
Hyalite
Lake

Emerald
Lake

Heather
Lake

N
W   E
S

Hyalite Lake.

Hyalite Lake (4 Paws Up!)

Distance: 11 miles round-trip
Time: 5–6 hours
Difficulty: Moderate

Overview

Something interesting always happens on this trail—it is known for late snow and fast-moving storms. That being said, it is an amazing hike that passes 11 waterfalls and ends at a beautiful alpine lake, perfect for a cooldown and some playtime in the water. If you are feeling energetic, it is just another 2 miles along an established trail to Hyalite Peak. If you are interested in doing this as a short backpacking trip, there are primitive campgrounds along the lake. Be prepared for weather, as well as bikes, horses, other dogs, and people on the trail, but if your dog is social and doesn't have problems with other trail users, this is a great hike!

Driving Directions

From Bozeman head to Hyalite Canyon Recreation Area by taking 19th Avenue going south. There will be a sign for Hyalite Canyon; take a left and travel about 11.5 miles to the reservoir (nice for a quick dog dip if it is hot). The road goes to the left around the reservoir. After the reservoir the road becomes dirt, and there is a sign indicating a right for the Hyalite Creek Trail. Follow that road for 2 miles until it ends at a large parking lot.

Hiking Directions (see map on page 53)

From the parking lot, follow signs for the Hyalite Creek Trail and Grotto Falls. This first 1.5 miles is handicapped accessible and great for small children—not too hard, and a beautiful waterfall is at the end. After Grotto Falls you continue to follow gradual switchbacks for the next 4 miles to the lake.

This takes you through lodgepole, subalpine fir forest and great volcanic rock outcroppings with continual access to the creek. Along the way there are 10 more (yes, count them) waterfalls to visit (but watch your dog since there are steep drop-offs). After about 5 miles, there will be a signed junction. Take the east fork toward Hyalite Peak. From here, the lake is a short walk and a nice place to sit and take in views of alpine peaks, while having lunch and tossing sticks for your dog. The trail tends to hold its snow so you can find yourself post-holing even in June and/or getting snowed on in August, but it is worth the hike for waterfalls, the lake, high alpine wildflower meadows, and views. This hike definitely has something for everyone.

Milo's Notes: Just when I thought the heat was too much, we headed up, and I found snow, rivers, and a lake—all would have been perfect except for the little adventure I had in the fast-moving creek.

Doc's Notes: Even though this is long, it is gradual with a great lake at the end, and what can I say—it was pretty entertaining to watch Milo almost get swept away. Puppies!

Mace takes the climb to Hyalite Peak.

View from History Rock Trail.

History Rock

Distance: 2 miles up and back to the rock, 12 miles
through to South Cottonwood, or as long
as you want out and back
Time: 1–5 hours
Difficulty: Easy to moderate

Overview

History Rock is located in Hyalite Canyon, close enough to Bozeman for a quick dog jaunt, or, if you are feeling adventurous, you can
leave a car at South Cottonwood (see hike 23 for driving directions
to that trailhead) and hike through. The hike starts out in a meadow
filled with wildflowers and a few areas for a drink from the stream. The
route gradually progresses into the forest, and water is accessible but not
directly on the trail after the meadow. If you continue to South Cottonwood, there is a stretch of alpine meadow that does not have access
to water, but your dog will be happy once you descend into the South
Cottonwood drainage, where water and streams are once again plentiful.

History Rock is a fun destination to take in a bit of Gallatin Valley's
history and read the names of early settlers and visitors to the rock, as

57

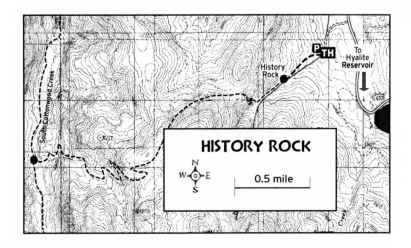

your dog rests under the shade of forest canopy. If you have time, the through hike to South Cottonwood is truly one of our favorites!

Driving Directions

From Bozeman head to Hyalite Canyon Recreation Area by taking 19th Avenue going south. At the sign for Hyalite Canyon, take a left (east) and travel about 10 miles. The parking lot is on the right and will be marked as History Rock—if you reach the reservoir, you have gone too far, and you will need to backtrack less than a mile to the parking lot.

Hiking Directions

From the parking lot follow the trail that goes through a meadow filled with wildflowers. It is great moose habitat, and from the frenzied activities of the dogs, it is a good bet there are chances for a wildlife encounter in this area. After about a quarter mile there is a sign to History Rock, and the trail climbs gently for the next three-quarters of a mile. After the rock, the trail becomes significantly steeper until you hit the ridge. If you choose to continue to South Cottonwood, follow the ridge, and signs will lead you through a stunning alpine meadow and then downhill to the South Cottonwood drainage. About halfway between History Rock and South Cottonwood the Forest Service has a small (two people but no limit on dogs!) cabin to rent (Fox Creek) if you want to extend your trip. There also is camping nearby in Hyalite Canyon.

Milo's Notes: Being a puppy I sometimes get a little freaked out with things I can't recognize quickly, like mountain bikes. There can be a lot of them on the trail, so I am getting used to it, but if your dog has problems with those metal things that go fast, you might want to try this midweek, when it isn't so crowded.

Doc's Notes: The through hike all the way to South Cottonwood leaves me sore and aching for days. I love the water, but I think it is better for me to do these as two different hikes. I like all the smells around History Rock—I wonder if those early dogs left their mark, as well?

Frieda and Milo, with Hyalite Reservoir in the background.

Hikers along Bozeman Creek.

Bozeman Creek

Distance: 1–12 miles, depending on where you turn around
Time: 30 minutes or longer
Difficulty: Easy to moderate

Overview

Bozeman dog lovers cannot beat this trail, which is actually a Forest Service road. It is close to town and makes for a great before-work, after-work, or even during-lunch hike. If you have time, the road goes for 10 miles up to Mystic Lake, but the first 3 miles to the outhouse are the most popular. There are a lot of hikers, runners, and mountain bikers, so make sure your dog is good with bicycles.

In addition, the road is groomed in winter for both skate and classic cross country skiing by the Bridger Ski Foundation, which makes a great winter surface for walking with your dog. Most winter walkers stick to the first mile due to the snow pack, but dogs are welcome to go along for a ski, and if the conditions are good, grooming goes all the way to Mystic Lake and sometimes over to Moser Creek in the Hyalite drainage. For more information about winter conditions, check the website bsfnordic.com to read the grooming report. Winter can be more congested than other seasons, with the cross country ski team practicing after school. This is a terrific, year-round trail through a wooded canyon following the creek.

Driving Directions

From Bozeman, take Kagy Boulevard east to Sourdough Road and turn south. Drive on Sourdough for 6 miles to Nash Road and turn right (west). Drive 0.5 miles on Nash Road to Bozeman Creek Road and turn left. Go 1.5 miles to the trailhead parking area.

Hiking Directions

The Forest Service road winds at a slight uphill along a creek and gets a bit steeper right before the 1-mile mark. Look for the mile markers along the right side of the trail, which let you keep track of

Milo thinks about a drink in Bozeman Creek.

mileage and make this a favorite route for runners. After the first mile you lose access to the stream, but there always seems to be water, albeit quite muddy, along the side of the road at regular intervals. There are ups and downs (mostly ups) for the next 2 miles. The willowy and riparian area makes it ideal moose country, and moose, along with other wildlife, often frequent the trail. Just before mile 3, once again there is a stream covert to refresh your buddy and an outhouse for you. This is the turnaround point for a nice downhill stroll to get a second look at the path. If you want to continue, the road levels out a bit and has incredible views as it meanders through the lodgepole forest and meets a bridge and another creek at 6 miles.

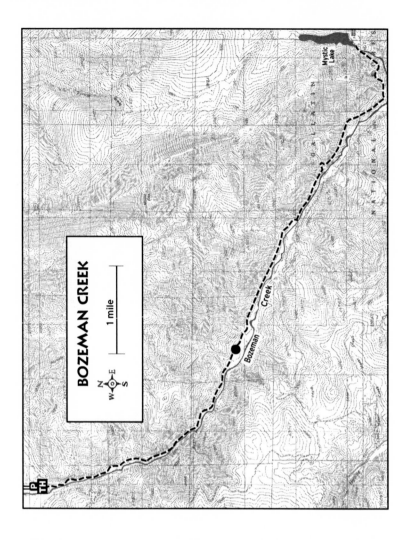

Milo's Notes: I love this downhill in the winter, I sometimes get going so fast trying to keep up with skiers that my back legs catch up to the front and I tumble. It is nice not to get snow caught in my paws and to be able to run along a hard surface in winter!

Doc's Notes: I have to be reminded not to jump into the Bozeman city water source, which is accessible within the first mile. There is a pool that makes up for it between mile 1 and the trailhead.

Milo takes a swim at Middle Cottonwood.

Middle Cottonwood

Distance: 4 miles round-trip or longer, depending
on turnaround point
Time: 2 hours
Difficulty: Easy to moderate

Overview

Easily accessible from Bozeman, this lovely and popular hike follows the Middle Cottonwood Creek drainage into the Bridger Mountains. There are multiple creek crossings and deep pools ideal for a doggie dip. The variety of forest and constant water make this a favorite. For the first ten minutes the trail is fairly open, but after the first creek crossing, you are covered by the forest as the creek wanders to a clearing that provides a view inside the hills. If you are one of those hikers who thinks that this is too close to town for bears... we're talking to you. There ARE black bears on this trail. We have the uncanny knack to see them regularly. Bring your spray or be "bear aware." Hikers usually post a note at the trailhead if they have seen one—so take a look before you head out.

Driving Directions

From Bozeman follow 19th Avenue north until you intersect Springhill Road. Take a right (north) on Springhill and proceed 1.7 miles to Sypes Canyon and turn right (east). Follow Sypes Canyon 1.5 miles and turn left on Summer Cutoff. Summer Cutoff winds around and ends at Saddle Mountain. Turn right (east) on Saddle Mountain Road and follow it for 1.8 miles. When Saddle Mountain looks like it dead ends, turn right, follow the road 1.3 miles (you go past a few houses right at the beginning) to the trailhead parking.

Hiking Directions

From the trailhead you'll cross the creek immediately and walk along the side of a hill for about a mile. The creek is out of view (but dogs usually find it) until the next stream crossing. From here the trail goes through a dense and lush forest following the creek on your left. A handful of deep pools will attract your pooch. Cross the third creek crossing on rocks and logs. In the spring, the creek can be flowing high and over the rocks. It's a cold barefoot dip but crossable. The trail will start a bit of a climb but also follows the creek closely. There is a really good dog pool on the right about five minutes past the third creek crossing—deep enough for a Milo and Doc to submerge.

About a half mile from there is a junction with a trail sign. If you choose to go right, you can take this trail to the Sypes Canyon Trail about 6 miles. This makes for a nice one-way if you leave a car at the Sypes Canyon trailhead, but be aware that there is very little water once you cross the creek.

Stay left at the junction, and the trail will climb and switchback steeply to the first clearing and view. Doc likes to turn around here. Milo likes to continue on. Walk the trail down the hill, and the creek will be on your right. You can continue for quite a while with the creek close by until you get to a large meadow. After that you are headed up Saddle Peak, and the trail gets steep with some scrambling up to the peak. This is suitable for mountain dogs, but make sure you carry some water.

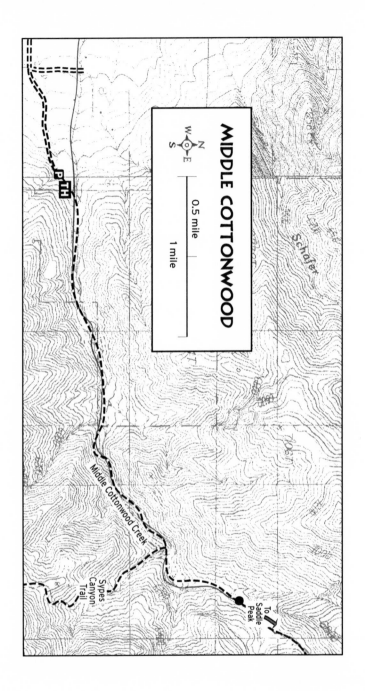

MIDDLE COTTONWOOD

N
W · E
S

0.5 mile

1 mile

Schafer

Middle Cottonwood Creek

Sypes
Canyon
Trail

To
Saddle
Peak

PTH

Wendy and Milo on the Middle Cottonwood Trail.

Milo's Notes: This hike is not a major panter. I like to continue on and follow the creek for a while.

Doc's Notes: This is the perfect quick mountain hike with something for everyone. Pools for me and wildflowers for you.

Truman Gulch in early spring.

Truman Gulch

Distance: 4 miles round-trip or longer, depending on turnaround point
Time: 2.5 hours
Difficulty: Moderate

Overview

The dogs really seemed to love this trail. We thought they were smiling as they ran up and down the trail, stopping at the several watering holes. This hike has a lot of potential: good water, a smooth, well-defined path, and nice views. The trail also is used frequently by mountain bikers and horses, and it is known to be inhabited by black bears (yes, we have seen them there). All and all, it makes for a good hike when you have a limited amount of time.

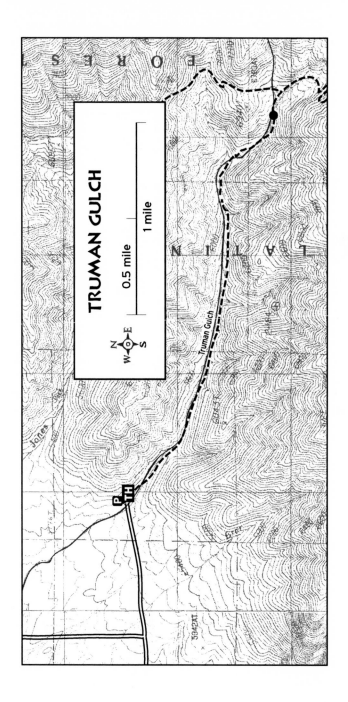

TRUMAN GULCH

0.5 mile

1 mile

N
W—E
S

69

Driving Directions

From Bozeman follow 19th Avenue to Springhill Road. Turn right (north) on Springhill and continue 8.5 miles to Springhill Community Road on the right. At the sign for Truman Gulch turn right and continue 1.6 miles to Walker Road. The Springhill Church is on the corner. Turn right and drive 1.1 miles to Forswall Road and turn left. Continue 3 miles to the trailhead parking area at road's end.

Hiking Directions

The trailhead is not marked with a sign, but if you follow Forswall road to the end, it will bring you to a parking lot and the Truman Gulch Trail. The trail is a straight shot through Truman Gulch with easy, steady elevation gain until about a mile in and then a climb that will have you breathing a little more heavily. The hike will bring you through a park-like lodgepole pine forest with steep hills on either side. The first 2 miles are lush with flora, including mountain maples, and in the spring it is thick with clematis and glacial lilies. The trail follows a stream and crosses it several times. The crossings are not difficult, but if you are a little unsteady on small rocks and in one case logs, hiking poles might be a nice idea. There is water the entire way, and even if it is sometimes out of view, it's always in earshot. After about an hour the trail gets steeper, but not for long. It will continue along the creek to a large meadow with a nice view of the Bridger Mountain ridgeline. This brings us to our turnaround point.

However, if you and your dog are feeling adventuresome, you can connect to the Bridger Mountains National Recreation Trail. This trail takes you along the ridge of the Bridger Mountains for 21 miles and accesses several of the Bridger Peaks. The terrain is suitable for active dogs, as long as you bring extra water, since water access becomes intermittent from this point.

Milo's Notes: It is my goal to move the largest stick or branches possible—there were some really big ones here to pull around. I also perfected the dog version of a hockey stop, spraying late spring snow in every direction.

Uma's Notes: The steep side hills were great to release some energy and still stay with the group.

South Cottonwood

Distance: 4 miles round-trip or longer,
depending on turnaround point
Time: 2 hours or longer,
depending on turnaround point
Difficulty: Easy to moderate

Overview

This trail is about a 20-minute drive from the center of Bozeman and gets you and your pooch into the foothills of the Gallatin Range. The majority of the hike is in a shaded area, making this a better hike for later in the season because the snow pack lingers. You and your dog could be post-holing well into May. It is a popular trail for trail runners and their hounds wanting a change from the runs in town. At times the creek is out of view, but it has a handful of crossings and pools for dips and drinks.

Driving Directions

Take Main Street west out of town and it will turn into Huffine Lane. Take this about 2 miles to Cottonwood Road and turn left (south). Take Cottonwood Road 7.5 miles to Cottonwood Canyon Road and turn left. Follow this for 2 miles to the trailhead at the end of the road.

Hiking Directions

The trail starts at the parking area. The first 20 minutes of the hike switches back and forth for a bit of uphill through the forest then levels out as you pass a gate and get to the creek. A log bridge provides the creek crossing, and this is the first watering hole. Once across the bridge there is a short climb and the trail continues to follow the creek, though sometimes it is out of sight. It goes for miles with a few changes in incline. If you take the trail to the second creek crossing, this is roughly 2 miles and a good turnaround point.

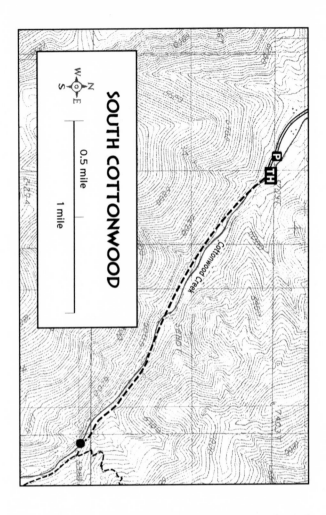

However, for those more eager, the trail goes on for miles and eventually connects to History Rock (see hike 19) in the Hyalite Mountains. The area definitely has black bears, so you might want to bring your bear spray. It can be buggy after the snowmelt, so remember the bug spray, too.

Doc, Milo, and Uma's Notes: Uma, Doc's best pal (sorry Milo), is an aggressive runner and likes this trail because she can go for miles with the slopes keeping her on the trail.

Tank walks the plank following Wendy.

Milo on top of Drinking Horse Trail.

Drinking Horse

Distance: 3.2-mile loop
Time: 1 hour
Difficulty: Moderate

Overview

Close enough to Bozeman, but not as crowded as the M Trail, the Drinking Horse Trail makes for a quick hike squeezed into a busy day for you and your dog. The trail has ample water from a stream at the base, but during the dog days of summer, it is best to hike this in the morning or evening. Intrinsik Architects of Bozeman designed a stunning bridge as a memorial to Kevin Mundy, a Bozeman native and ski patroller who died at age 26. The bridge crosses Bridger Creek toward the beginning or end of the round-trip hike and is a great place

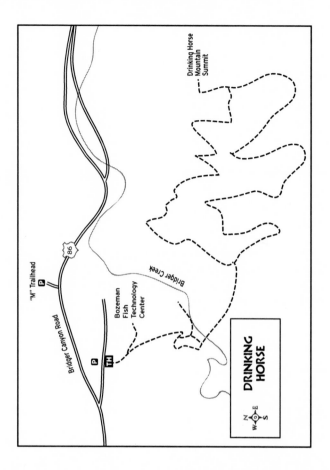

for dogs to cool off and play in the generally calm water. Nice views of the Absarokas, Crazies, and Gallatin Range can be seen from the summit. Look for some funky man-made shelters constructed from branches at the top.

Driving Directions

Drinking Horse is easily accessed from downtown Bozeman. From Main Street turn north on North Rouse (Route 86, the road to Bridger Bowl) and go 4.1 miles to the Bozeman Fish Technology Center access road on the right. The trailhead parking lot is to the left (north) of the access road and across from the popular M Trail.

Hiking Directions

From the parking lot follow the trail downhill until you reach the bridge that crosses Bridger Creek. After the bridge, the trail crosses a road, and then heads up a slope. There is a fork not far up the trail. To the right is a bit more gradual climb, although both ways primarily go up. The hike goes through mature cottonwoods by the stream and then up through a lodgepole forest. As you approach the summit, the trail weaves through an open meadow and then rocky outcroppings with overlooks at the top. The way down is steeper and switchbacks back to the fork in the trail, and then back to the bridge with an uphill hike to the parking lot.

Milo's Notes: There is a lot to explore in the woods through here, and I like chasing sticks in the river after a good hike. Sometimes, I think I could go further, or at least get another romp in after the hike, but if I get to chase sticks, life is good.

Doc's Notes: This is perfect for me. A nice walk with some good smells up to the summit, and on the way back I can lay down in the stream, cool off, and have a good drink all at the same time!

Milo on the bridge at the Drinking Horse Trail.

Etta along Hedvig's Trail.

Hedvig's Trail at Snowfill Dog Park

Distance: 1.25-mile loop
Time: 30 minutes or more
Difficulty: Easy

Overview

This popular dog park, located north of Bozeman, is a must for so-cial dogs and/or dogs that might wander too much. It is a good place to take your dogs if they are the type to run off, since very little can happen in this well-enclosed area.

Completed in 2008, this 37-acre, fenced park located on the old landfill and maintained by GVLT (Gallatin Valley Land Trust) has a variety of terrain and uses. Along the perimeter you can find Hedvig's Trail. This trail meanders up and down hills for 1.25 miles. The trail is dedicated to and funded in part by the friends of Hedvig Flowers, a local Nordic skier, hiker, and dog lover (Satch was her faithful Brittany Spaniel) who lost her battle with cancer in 2007. The area provides lovely views of the Bridger Mountains and surrounding farms.

77

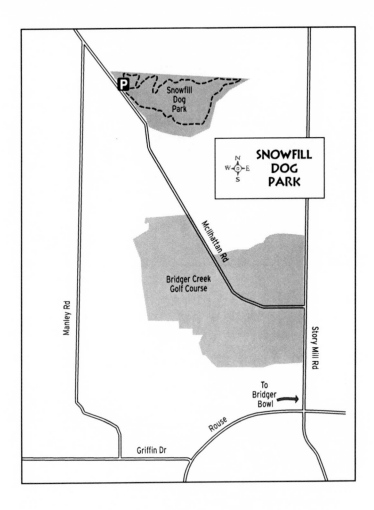

Snowfill is a multi-season park with sledding in the winter and hiking all year long. Warning: it can be a bit muddy in early spring, so bring a towel if you don't like dirty paws in your car. GVLT has installed a water pump by the entrance for your thirsty pal to cool off—many dogs and people hang out by the dog water cooler to socialize at the end of their hike. If you are lucky, you might come across the work of a local park user who decorates the trail on different occasions—look for potpourri along the trail, or decorations hung up on the fence celebrating different holidays or seasons.

Driving Directions

One way to Snowfill is to take Rouse (the road to Bridger Bowl) northwest to Story Mill, turn left (north) on Story Mill, and turn left again on McIlhattan. The Snowfill parking lot will be past the Bridger Creek Golf Course on your right. An alternate route (better in winter) is to take Rouse, then left on Griffin Drive, right on Manley past East Gallatin Ponds, and then right on McIlhatten—the Snowfill parking lot will be on your left.

Hiking Directions

Go through the gate and follow the trail to the right or left. To the right there will be a steady, but more gentle, climb; to the left it is a bit steeper. You can stop at several benches along the way to sit and rest and throw balls for the dog. Many people do several laps to get a longer walk or run in.

Milo's Notes: So many dogs—so little time. I love going up here, I get to steal other dog's balls, and no one seems to care. Everyone seems to love me here; I get lots of pets and greetings.

Doc's Notes: If I don't feel up to a long walk, this is the place to go. Sometimes I don't even go with the group, I just hang out by the water pump and greet the other dogs!

Milo gets a drink at the dog's water pump at Hedvig's Trail.

Peet's Hill/Burke Park

Distance: 2 miles round-trip
Time: 30 minutes or longer
Difficulty: Easy

Overview

Peet's Hill is a Bozeman institution. It is centrally located with multiple access points and has good terrain for walking and jogging and a nice slope for winter sledders. The area is leash-free and is the first leash-free park in Bozeman. It is a great location for a stroll and doggie social opportunity. The trail is 1 mile, one-way, with an easy uphill grade, and it provides great views of the Hyalite Mountains, Bridger Mountains, and the town of Bozeman.

Dogs run free in this grassy hilltop with well-worn trails. It connects to other arteries in the Bozeman trail system, so is well-used by joggers and commuters. In the winter the path continues to be popular and is usually very walkable. It has a loyal following, and many dog walkers come here regularly to socialize with other walkers and their dogs. Please bring bags to pick up after the pooch on this one.

Driving Directions

In Bozeman take Main Street to Church and turn south. Drive about 1 mile, and the small parking lot will be on your left. You can also park at the library if the lot is full. It can also be accessed by parking behind Bozeman Deaconess Hospital or at Lindley Park off East Main Street.

Hiking Directions

The trail starts at the end of the parking lot and has a quick and semi-steep climb. There are multiple paths that lead you to the top of the hill. Take the trail to the right to the top of the hill and pick up the main trail going right again. You will be heading south and facing the Hyalite Mountains. As you walk you will see the hospital off to your left in addition to the adult living facility. The field between the trail

Milo, Ula, and Etta enjoy a late fall day on Peet's Hill.

and hospital is groomed for Nordic skiing in the winter, however, dogs are not allowed on these ski trails. To your right you will see views of Montana State University, including the football stadium and sport fields. When you get to the top of the hill and the end of the trail, you

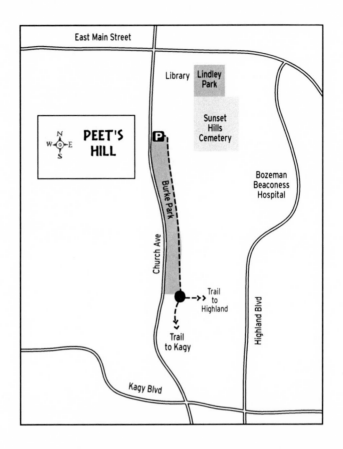

can choose to continue on straight or go left to connect to new trails to add mileage, which is great for runners, but this is the end of the leash-free area. You can loop around to your right, which will bring you back to the main trail, and you can follow your path back the way you came. If you prefer to skip the steep uphill, consider starting at Lindley Park or behind the hospital.

Milo's Notes: I love when Aunt Becky takes me here, because we can jog together and she doesn't have to leash me up. She still can't keep up with me.

Doc's Notes: Lots of social opportunities, and there is usually a nice Golden gal for me to sniff. What can I say, I like the ladies.

Milo takes one last swim for the year in the pond at Bozeman's Regional Park.

Bozeman Regional Park
(also called the 100 Acre Park)

Distance: 1–2 miles
Time: 0.5–1 hour
Difficulty: Very easy

Overview

Although this area wouldn't technically be considered a dog hike, the Regional Park in Bozeman is leash-free and has a network of trails along with two ponds for your furry friend to cool off in. The park also boasts the dinosaur playground, which is a great stop for families that want an outing that has something for everyone.

Driving Directions

The Regional Park's main parking lot is off Oak Street. Take 19th Avenue north from downtown, turn left at the signal at 19th and Oak. Proceed 1.2 miles until you see an unpaved parking lot on the right.

Hiking Directions

Starting from the parking lot there are several trail options, with all of them interconnecting and bringing you back to the parking lot. The area is completely flat with one man-made hill that is used for sledding in the winter. Dogs are allowed in the ponds (and many use them) so this is a great place on those really hot days to cool off your pooch either after a hike, or to just get him out for a quick swim or ball chase. This park is perfect for very social dogs; you can often find other dogs chasing balls either in the fields or swimming after them in the ponds. There are probably more chuck-its per acre here than any other place in Montana. Recently, picnic tables have been added by the pond, which makes a nice place to sit and visit with other dog owners as your dog shakes on unwitting bystanders.

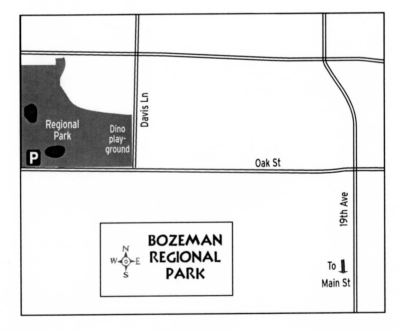

Etta enjoys a fall day at Bozeman's Regional Park.

Milo's Notes: I get so excited coming here that I usually forget to actually retrieve my ball and often lose sight of it. Fortunately, I am not the only dog to do this, so I usually find another one to replace it. I wish I could go over and visit the kids at the playground, but I need a leash for that.

Doc's Notes: There is a nice covered bridge to sit and cool off under if I get tired of chasing balls and swimming. I love the variety of dogs I can play with.

Tank's Notes: When I visit Milo in the summer, this is great place to burn off a bit of Lab energy in the evenings!

Becky and Wendy's Notes: This park is well used and has bags for poop pickup at the parking lot. Please make sure to clean up after your dog, so dogs can continue to be welcome here!

Butte and Helena Region

Uma and Doc take a break to enjoy the Pintler Wilderness.

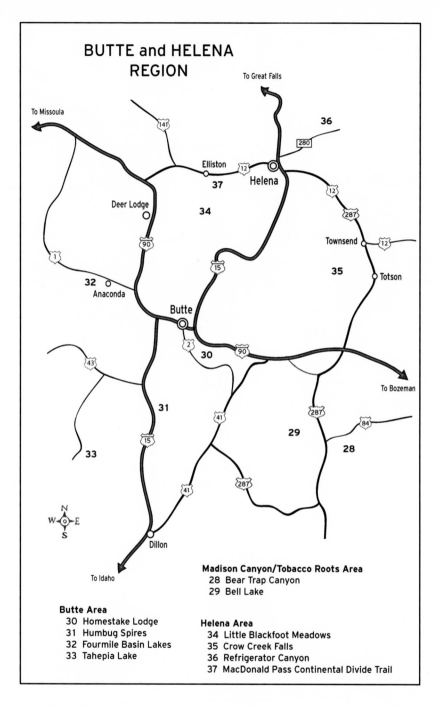

BUTTE and HELENA REGION

To Great Falls

36

280

To Missoula

141

Elliston

37

12

Helena

12

Deer Lodge

34

287

90

Townsend

12

1

35

Totson

32

Anaconda

15

Butte

2

30

90

To Bozeman

43

31

41

287

84

15

29

28

33

287

41

Dillon

N
W E
S

To Idaho

Madison Canyon/Tobacco Roots Area
28 Bear Trap Canyon
29 Bell Lake

Butte Area
30 Homestake Lodge
31 Humbug Spires
32 Fourmile Basin Lakes
33 Tahepia Lake

Helena Area
34 Little Blackfoot Meadows
35 Crow Creek Falls
36 Refrigerator Canyon
37 MacDonald Pass Continental Divide Trail

The Madison River as it carves its way through the canyon.

Bear Trap Canyon

Distance: 1–8 miles, depending on where you turn around
Time: 30 minutes or longer
Difficulty: Easy

Overview

A trail that follows the ebbs and flows of the Madison River is hard to pass up. The high country desert setting makes this prime rattlesnake country, so this trail is only advisable in the winter and spring. It is well used by hikers, joggers, and anglers alike, therefore the trail is worn all year long and stays surprisingly dry. It is a terrific option for those in the area looking to wear down the pets with some mileage and get winter bath as well.

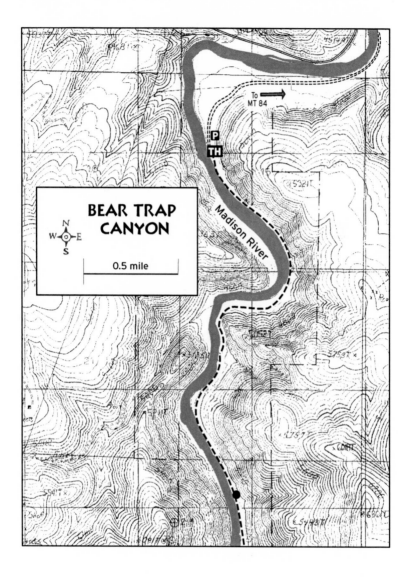

If you are also in the need for a soak, check out Water of the Gods Hot Springs, which is a bit farther west, right after you turn off Route 84 and onto Route 287. Adding a hot springs visit completes the outing, maybe not for the doggies, but it is your day, too.

Driving Directions

From Bozeman, take Main Street west, which turns into Huffine Lane. Once at Four Corners, continue west and toward Norris, and the road turns into Montana Road 84, a.k.a. Norris Road. Follow this 30 miles to the Bear Trap Recreational Area. Turn left on the dirt road and follow this to the end, about 3.2 miles.

Hiking Directions

The hike begins at the parking lot and follows the river the entire way. The first eighth of a mile is a man-made pebble trail that is really inviting for joggers, and then the trail turns into a semi-rocky dirt path. It is easy hiking, and it curves ever so slightly, following the curves of the river through the canyon. The canyon walls and sagebrush landscape complement the beauty of the river. You are certain to run into fly fishermen in the first couple miles, since this area lends itself to great wade fishing. We like to take the hike about 2 miles to the top of a small hill. The path continues for about 6 more miles if you need more action for the pack, but we like to turn around here for a beverage and snack in order to make time for a soak.

A special treat is to head to the Water of the Gods Hot Springs after the hike, but make sure to check their hours of operation before you go so you won't be disappointed if it is closed.

Milo's Notes: I always see some people jogging and love to challenge their speed! See if they can keep up with me. It is so tempting to join the fishermen in the river, but Doc always reminds me that it is not good manners—ah yes, *multiuse* is the word of the day.

Doc's Notes: Great cardio for the old ticker, with not too much stress on the bones. I am way asleep by the time we get back to the paved road.

Bell Lake invites canine swims.

Bell Lake

Distance: 6 miles round-trip
Time: 4 hours
Difficulty: Strenuous

Overview

This oasis of a lake is straight up 2,000 feet for 3 miles, with an end elevation of 9,000 feet. You will never have to scramble, but you will definitely earn your trail mix and rawhides after this hike. There are just a few (and just enough) water stops along the way, though you hear the creek rushing nearby. If you have a very thirsty hound or you are an overly protective (we understand you) dog parent, bring an

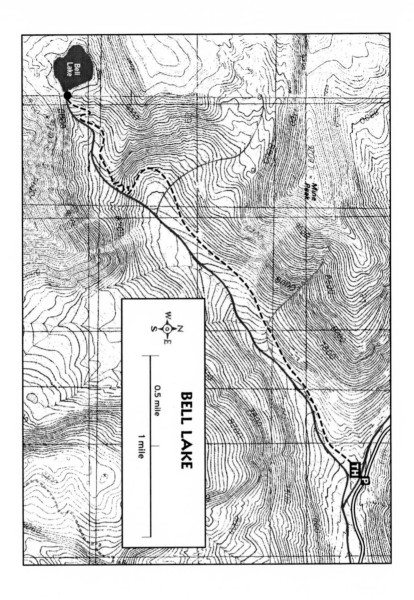

extra bottle of water for Fido. The lake is sure to please and to refresh your hound. Bring a rod if you are an angler; we saw many rising fish. Also, if there isn't a mountain breeze, we found it fairly buggy at the lake even in early August.

Driving Directions

You can get to Pony either via Norris or Three Forks on Route 287. Once in Pony, turn on South Willow Creek Road. Take this about 2 miles to the sign to the Potosi Hot Springs Campground and turn right. The campground is a little over 6 miles away. Drive past the campground (both north and south loops) and continue on the "Primitive Road" (fine condition) for 2.7 miles to the Bell Lake trailhead.

Hiking Directions

The hike has steady climbs and traverses from the trailhead. After a few fragrant sage fields and forest switchbacks, about 2 miles into the hike, you'll come to a trail sign marking pedestrian traffic only. Take this trail to the right, and it will switchback through the white bark pine forest across an old rocky road. There are a few false summits on this hike. The last mile has the most climbs. The lake spreads across 18 acres, and you will have a view of Thompson Peak.

Milo's Notes: I loved the uphills and being able to run through the fields—I had plenty of energy left to swim and chase sticks at the lake, but I was ready for a long nap back in the car!

Doc's Notes: I felt my age once at the top, but the plethora of sticks to chew and swimming made up for the work.

Milo and Doc test the creek waters.

93

Follow the paws!

Homestake Lodge/Busy Beaver Trail

Distance: 4-mile loop or longer with connecting trails
Time: 2 hours or more
Difficulty: Easy

Overview

The best way to describe this location is Disneyland for Dogs. It has everything a dog desires: wide open fields, streams, woods filled with sticks, and well-placed ponds for a quick swim. Izzy, the resident dog, is happy to tag along and serve as a tour guide, pointing the way to the best smells and watering holes this area has to offer.

Homestake Lodge is a private cross-country ski resort at the top of Homestake Pass. Chris and Mandy Axelson, the owners, have graciously made their trails available (but please no dogs in the lodge) at no charge for summer use by mountain bikers and hikers. They are happy to have dogs and people enjoying their summer trails but ask visitors to check in at the lodge and to be courteous to the various user groups (weddings, camps, family reunions) that have rented out the lodge for the day. If you are thinking about making a weekend of it to do some real exploring of the area, Homestake Lodge has several different lodging options, ranging from dormitory rooms in the lodge to more private yurts, cabins, and a campground. Best of all, the resort is dog-friendly and has several specified groomed cross-country ski trails that welcome you and your buddy for a winter adventure. For more information on the lodge, you can visit their website: www. homestakelodge.com.

Driving Directions

Homestake Lodge is located 3 miles off the I-90 Homestake Pass exit. From the exit go to the south side of I-90 and turn onto FS 240. This will be straight off the ramp coming from the Butte direction, and it will be a right off the ramp and then a left turn after crossing over the interstate coming from the Bozeman direction. FS 240 road is in the opposite direction from Homestake Lake/Campground and Lake Delmoe. Drive down FS 240 for 3 miles. After 3 miles, you will go under the big electrical transmission lines, and there will be a road on your right. This will be the road into Homestake Lodge.

Hiking Directions

From the parking lot, head up the stairs to the lodge to get a map and ask Chris or Mandy for the best hiking or biking options (if they are not there, there are maps posted at many intersections, or you can download one from their website).

A good option is to follow the Busy Beaver Trail. The hike starts out along a well-maintained forest road. It crosses areas with lots of water, great for a dog dip, but you might also want some insect repellent for yourself. Keep following signs for the Busy Beaver Trail, and you will find yourself walking through aspen groves intermingled with the Boulder Batholith (large rock formations). If you lose the trail, just follow the signs back to the lodge, since all of the trails head back there eventually. Once at the lodge, take some time to sit back and enjoy your lunch on the deck—it's not often that you get to sit at a table after a day of hiking.

Milo's Notes: I was here in the winter, and I love running really fast to keep up with the skiers. Things are different in the summer, and there are lots more smells.

Doc's Notes: Uma and I got to sniff and swim while Milo was entertained by Izzy, the resident dog—nothing too steep, and the wide cross-country trails were fun to run on.

Homestake Lodge in the distance.

Moose Creek.

Humbug Spires (4 Paws Up!)

Distance: 6 miles round-trip
Time: 3 hours
Difficulty: Easy to moderate

Overview

If you and Fido are looking for a uniquely scenic hike near the Butte area, Humbug Spires is a great choice. It follows a tributary of the Big Hole River, Moose Creek, to unusual granite outcroppings in the Boulder Mountains. The spires, some of which tower a few hundred feet, are a large attraction for rock climbers. The hike provides a variety of flora, including the willowy creekside and sparsely popu-

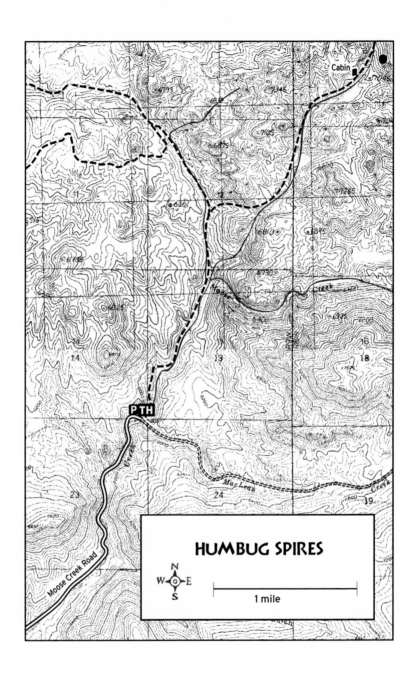

HUMBUG SPIRES

1 mile

lated pine forests peppered with a few grassy meadows. The creek and its forks provide plenty of water for the pups along the way.

Driving Directions

From Butte, drive south on I-15 25 miles to Exit 99, Moose Creek Road. Go south on the gravel Moose Creek Road 3 miles to the trailhead parking lot.

Hiking Directions

The trail starts just below the trail sign below the parking area. The path follows Moose Creek, with views of its willows and shrubs that make an ideal habitat for its namesake moose. Continue to stroll through a few meadows and woods along the creek. There are plenty of opportunities for your dogs to find new sticks to chew and chomp along the way. After about a mile and a half, the trail leaves the creek and climbs a bit. You will come across the remains of a miner's log cabin. Continue to hike the last, but steeper, mile and a half to reach The Wedge, which is one of the more pronounced outcroppings.

Milo's Notes: I love finding random sticks along the way. The last climb was a good one, but I loved the downhill relief back to the creek.

Uma's Notes: For a surly bird dog like myself, it was a great place for a good run and no bird scents to distract me from the sights. Just enough gain to work off the extra biscuits, but not too hard on my swollen joints.

The Wedge

Milo leads the hounds on the trail to Fourmile Basin Lakes.

Fourmile Basin Lakes

Distance: 8 miles round-trip
Time: 4 hours
Difficulty: Easy to moderate

Overview

This is a beautiful hike that gives you views of the snowcapped Anaconda Range, while making it to a clear and stunning alpine lake. The trail follows the creek, which, in early run-off season, can be flowing rapidly. The lake is fishable, so bring your rod.

Driving Directions

From Anaconda, drive 10 miles west on Montana Highway 1 toward Spring Hill. Turn south on Twin Lakes Creek Road (FR 5131), which is not well marked. It is just past the Warm Springs Campground and between mile markers 19 and 20. Once on Twin Lakes Creek road, stay to your left (not veering toward the picnic area) and go 3.5 miles. You can park here or continue 0.5 miles up FR 171 to the trailhead.

Hiking Directions

Follow the signs for Trail 44, which follows a Forest Service road along Twin Lakes Creek drainage. After the first mile the creek is out of sight for a while as you walk steadily up the road, and there is a large pond (or small lake) on the left for a good drink and cool-off. The road will continue to switchback for the next 2 miles then ends at a trail. Follow the trail for the last mile through dark timber to the lake.

Milo's Notes: I like hiking on the road. It lets me be side by side with Wendy and Becky.

Doc's Notes: I liked exploring some of the side roads, but to get to the lake, stay on the main road the entire time.

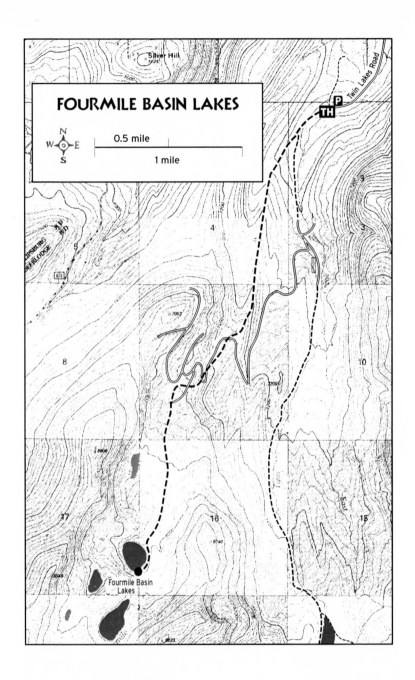

FOURMILE BASIN LAKES

N
W E
S

0.5 mile

1 mile

Silver Hill

Twin Lakes Road

TH P

Fourmile Basin
Lakes

Trail to Tahepia Lake.

Tahepia Lake/Mono Creek

Distance: 16 miles round-trip
Time: 8 hours
Difficulty: Moderate to strenuous

Overview

Sometimes you just have to do it—push yourself and your dog a little farther than usual to find some spectacular peaks surrounding a high alpine lake. If you are in the mood for a challenge, then Tahepia Lake, nestled in the Pioneer Mountains north of Dillon, is the perfect fit. Tahepia Lake can be accessed from the Mono Creek Campground along the Pioneer Scenic Byway. This is a relatively low-use area, so

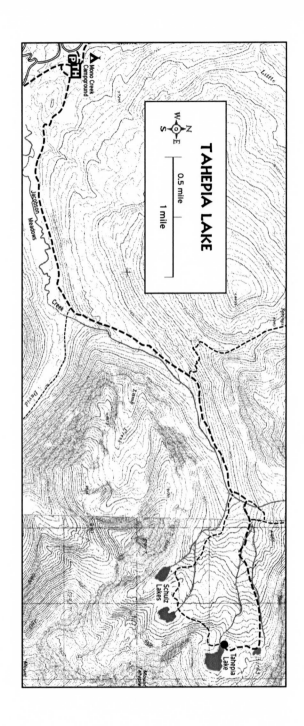

plan on spending a couple of nights at the campground if you want an early start and a more relaxing post-hike evening. You can also visit the interesting ghost town of Coolidge near the campground before you head out.

Driving Directions

The Pioneer Mountains Scenic Byway is found in the town of Wise River, 12 miles west of I-15 on Montana 43 from the Divide interchange on I-15 between Butte and Dillon. The actual Scenic Byway intersection in Wise River is not particularly well marked, however it is the only paved road going south from the town of Wise River. Mono Creek Campground is 22 miles south on a paved road. Take Forest Road 2465 southeast 1 mile to the campground. There are five designated sites at the campground; the trailhead is on the left and is well marked just before you get to the campground.

Mountain bikers take a side trip from the Tahepia Lake Trail up to Coolidge ghost town.

Hiking Directions

The trail starts out by crossing a beautiful meadow filled with lush grasses, wildflowers and abundant water, just perfect to get your dog ready for a somewhat strenuous climb up to the lake. Along the way are large boulders peeking out in odd formations, making the forest portion of this hike quite scenic and geologically interesting. At 2.5 miles the trail splits, with the right turn going to Torrey Peak—for Tahepia Lake you will want to continue left for another 5.5 miles. The 8-mile-long trail gains 2,400 feet and eventually drops you off at one of the most scenic high alpine lakes in all of western Montana. The trail follows Jacobson Creek the entire way, so your dog will always have access to water. Once at the lake, take some time for a game of fetch, if you have the energy, but be careful to watch for afternoon thunderstorms and turn around if the weather becomes threatening.

Milo's Notes: I even felt tired after this. It was great to curl up in the tent and have a good long snooze when we got down.

Doc's Notes: I stayed home and watched the cats in the neighborhood for this one; my old bones would have ached for days.

Tahepia Lake.

Uma prefers the bridge, while Doc is a natural at wading.

Little Blackfoot Meadows

Distance: 8 miles round-trip to the meadow
Time: 4 hours
Difficulty: Easy to moderate (for the length)

Overview

If it weren't for the length and a few steady uphills, this hike would seem more like a stroll through a shady, lush green park than a hike in the wilderness. The Little Blackfoot Meadows Trail is a gently sloped path that follows a clear and steady moving river for 4 miles until it unfolds into a large alpine meadow. Well-spaced lodgepole pines interspersed with deep green kinnikinnick, along with the sound of moving water, make this a great day out for you and your dog.

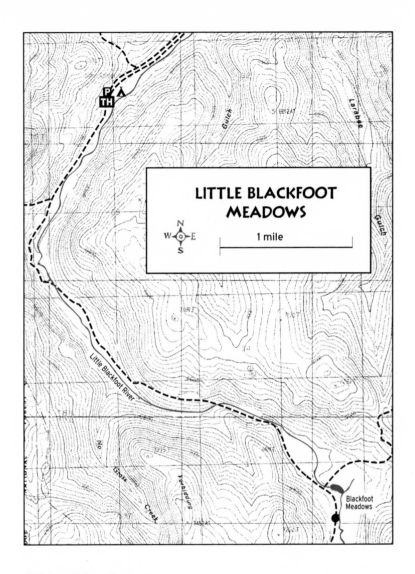

Driving Directions

From Helena drive west on Montana Highway 12 toward Missoula. About 17 miles out of Helena (and 1 mile before Elliston), you will see a sign for Little Blackfoot and FS 227; turn left. The road goes for 12 miles with the first 3 miles being paved and the remaining 9 miles a well-maintained dirt road. After you pass the Kading Campground on the left and Kading cabin on the right, the road ends with a trailer turnaround and parking before designated signs.

Hiking Directions

For the first mile, the trail is actually a very pretty Jeep road. There is evidence of some horse and mountain bike use, but it looked like very light use. The road follows the Little Blackfoot River with lots of opportunities for dog swims along the way. Once the road turns into a trail, there are some well-maintained bridges to cross the river, and a few tributary stream crossings along the way. The trail is generally flat as it winds through a lush forest covered with kinnikinnick (a deep green ground cover).

After 3 miles there is another river crossing that makes for a nice spot to rest and have a snack. The meadow is a mile past the bridge with a few uphill sections. The sidecuts and meadows give a nice variety to the terrain and let you know that you and your buddy deserve that trail mix and dog biscuit once you reach the meadow.

Milo's Notes: One word for this trail: *SQUIRRELS!*

Doc's Notes: I loved how it never got too hot, and there was lots of water to drink and cool off in.

Uma's Notes: The trees were so well spaced I could sniff and roam and still be in sight of the trail.

Milo stops to check out the forest.

Crow Creek Falls (4 Paws up!)

Distance: 6 miles round-trip
Time: 3 hours
Difficulty: Easy to moderate

Overview

The diverse Elkhorn Mountains are a little treasure in big country. These mountains can easily be overlooked by recreationalists, since other nearby ranges have more majestic snowcapped peaks. This recreation and wildlife area is near Helena, and the Crow Creek Falls is a terrific destination, with plenty of dog swimming holes and a variety of terrain in just a few miles. There are a handful of trailheads that can access the Crow Creek Trail and as many methods of reaching them. We like the Jump Off Trailhead and found the easiest access is south of the town of Townsend via the town of Toston.

Driving Directions

From Helena drive south on Montana Highway 287 past Townsend to Toston and turn right, going west on County Road 285. Take this 10 miles to the town of Radersburg. As you drive through the small town, the road turns into a dirt road now called Crow Creek Road 424. The road is rough in patches, but manageable the entire way. Drive 15 miles on the dirt road to the trailhead turnoff. The turnoff to the trailhead is marked with a sign on the right that says Crow Creek Trail 109 and is 2 miles past a junction and sign for the Eagle Guard Station. When you turn into the parking area for the trailhead it is signed as the Jump Off Trailhead.

Hiking Directions

The trail starts off very easy with a downhill approach, switching back and forth down to the creek. In the spring, the water is likely to be moving rapidly. The trail leaves the creek briefly then takes you to a sturdy footbridge crossing. After crossing the bridge you will be following the roar of the creek for a good mile through a variety of

Crow Creek Falls roar.

terrain, including lush growth and boulder fields. After the mile the trail takes you away from the creek up the first real climb. The top of the climb brings you to an open meadow full of sagebrush. The trail is marked, but be sure to go left. The trail widens and goes back to the

111

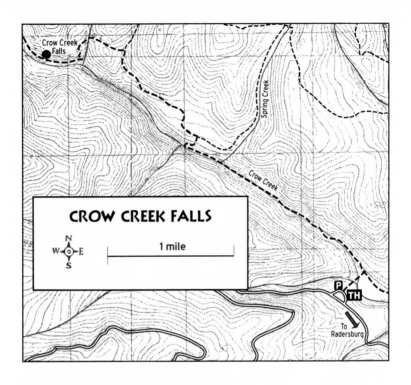

woods. Though Crow Creek is out of sight, there are smaller creeks that intersect the path for dog-drinking opportunities.

The last half mile of the trail winds around, and you can hear the roar of the falls—they are especially boisterous early in the season. The last yards are a steep downhill to the falls and creek. This is the only moderately strenuous stretch of the hike. The falls create some nice pools for a doggie dip, and there are logs and fire rings for a nice rest before the steep climb out.

Milo's Notes: I liked checking out the old mining shaft next to the falls.

Doc's Notes: This was like a spa. A little fitness, a little dip, more fitness, ah, another dip.

Uma's Notes: No birds in my radar on this hike, if only I got credit for pointing white-tailed deer.

Doc and Milo have a dip and sip at the base of Crow Creek Falls.

Refrigerator Canyon

Distance: 16 miles round-trip to Bear Prairie
Time: 8–9 hours
Difficulty: Moderate to strenuous (for distance)

Overview

Although this is long day hike, it is well worth the trip, even if you only do a portion of it and turn around before you reach Bear Prairie. The canyon alone merits a hike. It is an unusual hike for Montana, with its 200-foot limestone walls and vegetation that manages to survive even in harshest of environments. On a hot day, the canyon truly is cooler than surrounding areas, due to its narrow confines that trap cool breezes generating from the stream that runs right through the middle of the canyon and the trail. After the canyon area, water can be spotty, so if you choose to go farther, bring some extra water for your dog just in case.

Driving Directions:

Travel 16 miles east of Helena on State Highway 280 to York. At the York Bar, turn left (north) for 8 miles on County Road 4 to Nelson (the cribbage capital of the world), then turn right (east) toward Hogback Mountain, and go approximately 4 miles to the signed trailhead.

Hiking Directions

From the parking lot there is a slight climb into the canyon. Here you follow, or at times actually walk through, the stream. As you hike through the canyon, watch your footing, since there are lots of loose rocks and stream crossings. Once you leave the canyon, the trail becomes a well-maintained path that is generally shaded and pleasant walking. A bit past the canyon, the trail switchbacks and leads up to some nice views of Sheep and Candle Mountains.

After 3 miles there is a trail junction; Trail 252 heads right toward Porcupine Creek, but if you're hiking to Bear Prairie, stay left on Trail

114

Refrigerator Canyon.

259. This is a good turnaround for a shorter day hike. From the junction, the trail gradually flattens out, and Bear Prairie is another 5 miles.

Milo's Notes: I got so excited, I ran ahead up on top of one of the cliffs and knocked a rock off—it almost hit Wendy on the head. A good reminder that even on a day hike, accidents can happen.

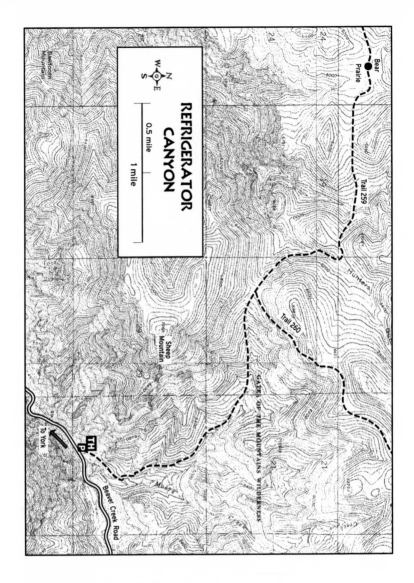

Doc's Notes: The 3-mile turnaround was perfect for me. Ah, to be young again.

Meadow on MacDonald Pass Trail.

Trail #37

MacDonald Pass Continental Divide Trail

Distance: 7 miles
Time: 4 hours
Difficulty: Easy to moderate

Overview

We would not travel out of our way to this trail, however, it is a is a good stop if you are traveling along Route 12 or are in the Helena area and are looking for a nice long hike that is not too strenuous. The trail starts at the top of MacDonald Pass. Therefore, most of the elevation gain occurs driving up to the trailhead. There is a very pretty mountain meadow about 3 miles into the hike, with great views of the surrounding area. Be forewarned, however, that there is very little water along the way, so you will need to bring extra for your dog if it is a hot day.

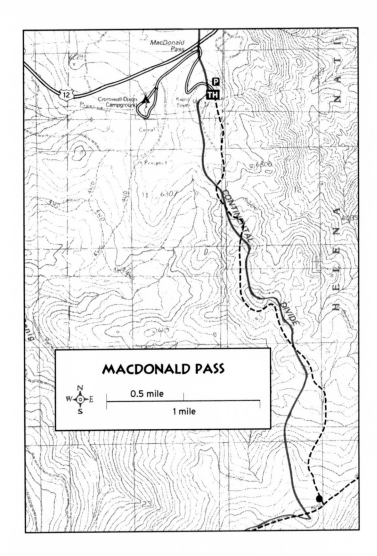

Driving Directions

At the top of MacDonald Pass look for signs to the Cromwell Dixon Campground. Turn into the campground road, and then take a quick left following signs for the CDT No. 348 (also sometimes known as the CDNST, Continental Divide National Scenic Trail). The trailhead is immediately to the right once you turn, but parking is a bit past it (you will see a Forest Service outhouse).

Hiking Directions

The trail begins through a burn area that is starting to regenerate. It continues with some terrain variation, but primarily it's a steady, slight uphill slope. The majority of the hike is through lodgepole pine, lush with wildflowers and the occasional boulder field. There are a few swampy areas that are crossed by boardwalks—this is the only water for your dog before you get into a long stretch of forest. After about 3 miles you will come to a large mountain-top meadow. There is livestock grazing in this area, so a few cows could be roaming around and more than a few cow patties (see Milo's Notes). Once in the meadow look for a CDT sign on the ridge. At that sign look to the west across the meadow to continue. This is our turnaround point, where you can take in the view, have a snack, and turn around to follow your path back. The trail continues across the Continental Divide, so you can hike as long as you want!

Milo's Notes: I just couldn't resist. Fresh cow manure—had to roll in it. For some reason Wendy and Becky did not seem too happy with me.

Wendy and Becky's Notes: We managed to hike down with a really smelly dog to the campground where, alas, there was no working water. We poured our drinking water over him, toweled Milo off with paper towels, and got him to the Little Blackfoot River for a final rinse—if you are hiking this trail, beware of fresh cow patties!

Wendy reacts to Milo after his roll in the cow manure.

Missoula Region

Tank and Milo come back to the trail from the Clark Fork River.

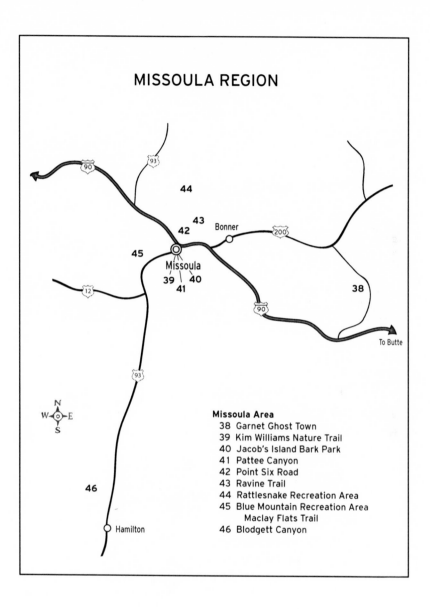

MISSOULA REGION

90

93

44

43
42   Bonner

200

45

Missoula
39 \ 40
41

12

38

90

To Butte

93

N
W ⬥ E
S

Missoula Area
38 Garnet Ghost Town
39 Kim Williams Nature Trail
40 Jacob's Island Bark Park
41 Pattee Canyon
42 Point Six Road
43 Ravine Trail
44 Rattlesnake Recreation Area
45 Blue Mountain Recreation Area
       Maclay Flats Trail
46 Blodgett Canyon

46

Hamilton

Garnet Ghost Town.

Garnet Ghost Town (leashed-only area)

Distance: Varies
Time: 1–2 hours
Difficulty: Easy

Overview

For a change of pace and a different type of dog adventure, try Garnet Ghost Town, just a short drive from Missoula. For a small fee ($3 per person but dogs are free) this well-preserved ghost town is dog-friendly as long as you keep your pet on a leash. There are water bowls set out for your pooch, and dogs are welcome to explore the old buildings and take a sniff inside the visitor's center if they want. There are several good hikes in the area, if you and your dog still need to stretch your legs after exploring the town, so take a picnic, grab a map at the visitor's center, and make a day of it.

Driving Directions

The best way to access Garnet Ghost Town is off Route 200, 30 miles east of Missoula. Turn south on the Garnet Range Road between mile markers 22 and 23. Follow the Garnet Range Road 11 miles (some of it is paved, the rest is well-maintained gravel road) to the parking lot.

If you are looking for some excitement, you can also access the area from I-90 by taking either the Drummond or Bearmouth exit. Then follow the north side frontage road to Bear Gulch Road, which is located 10 miles west of Drummond or 5 miles east of Bearmouth. Approximately 7.5 miles up Bear Gulch Road is the Cave Gulch Road Junction. From here, Garnet and the parking lot are 3 miles up Bear Gulch or 4 miles up Cave Gulch. This road is pretty primitive, narrow and rocky, but it does add to the adventure for the day.

Milo takes a drink from the dog-friendly fountain.

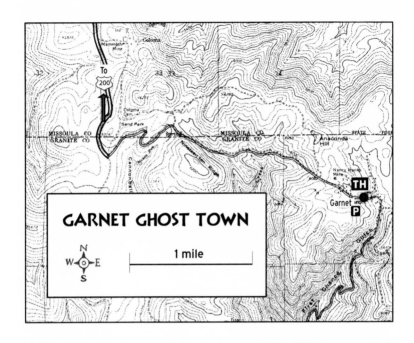

Hiking Directions

It is a short walk from the parking lot to Garnet. Heading downhill there is an overlook that lets you get your bearings, as you can see most of the town. The trail then enters the main street of the town. Several drinking fountains with dog bowls are along the main street. Stop in at the visitor's center for some information for a self-guided walk or join a tour to really explore this area.

Milo's Notes: I didn't want to go into the Old Well's Hotel—I thought I heard footsteps, but no one else was there. I liked smelling around the other buildings and searching out dog scents from a time gone by.

Doc's Notes: I liked this hike, lots of places to stop, sniff, and be petted.

Liz with Milo and Tank along the Kim Williams Trail.

Kim Williams Nature Trail

Distance: 2.5 miles
Time: 1–2 hours
Difficulty: Easy

Overview

For a nice, easy hike, perfect for all abilities of dogs and people, the Kim Williams Nature Trail in Missoula can't be beat. This trail follows an old abandoned railroad bed along the Clark Fork River. The trail is shared with other dog walkers, runners, and cyclists, so if your dog is the type to follow others or play Russian roulette with bicycles, best to keep him on a leash for the popular walk. There are plenty of side trails that lead down to the river for a quick dip and drink, or if you are feeling motivated, you can access Mt. Sentinel and the Hellgate Canyon Trail for a longer loop. Be aware that dogs need to be leashed for the first 300 yards of the trail.

Driving Directions

There are two approaches to the Kim Williams Nature Trail. If you are coming from I-90, exit at Van Buren Street and go south toward Broadway. Cross Broadway and find a parking spot (you can park near Missoula Chamber of Commerce on Front Street) and from there take the pedestrian bridge south toward the university and turn left after Jacob's Island, where you will see the trail.

If you are coming from Missoula, you can also access the park from the university side, near the Grizzly Stadium. In this case, before you cross the pedestrian bridge, turn right to access the trail.

Hiking Directions

At the start of the trail, you will see a sign to keep dogs on leash— this is for the first 300 yards only, but it is at times a congested trail, and if your dog is not great around people, bikes, and other trail users, it is not a bad idea to leash your dog for a while.

The trail follows the Clark Fork River, with lots of large cottonwood trees to shade parts of the path as you go, but in general it's open and sunny. After about 20 minutes look to your right for a spring, which is a great place for a quick drink for your dog without going down to the river. Right before the 3-mile mark (don't be fooled, you haven't actually hiked 3 miles, the markers start earlier along the path than you did) there is a path on the left going down to the river. This leads to a nice swimming area (the river is channeled) and gives another trail option that goes through the cooler woods and has easier access to the river. There are a few transient campsites along here, so if this makes you nervous, it is best to be with others if you take this trail.

Milo's Notes: I got a little thirsty on a hot day here, but a quick run down to the river fixed me up.

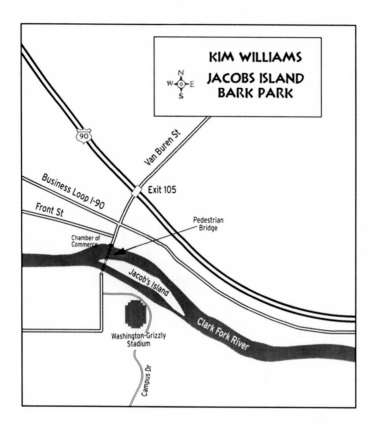

Rebecca the Chihuahua's Notes: I got to visit Missoula with my foster family. I am so lucky to have landed with people who like to walk dogs, what a great program for pets like me to have a place to go until I get adopted!

Milo, Petey, and Tank meet up for a drink at Jacob's Island Bark Park.

Jacob's Island Bark Park

Distance: Less than a mile
Time: However long you want
Difficulty: Easy

Overview

Even though this is not exactly a hike and more like a stroll, Jacob's Island deserves mention in a book about dogs. This dog park, surrounded by the Clark Fork River in the middle of Missoula, is Dog Eden! It's a 6-acre, leash-free, fenced area, with trees, shrubs, and slow-moving water, and best of all, lots of other dogs. It is long enough for a short sniff and wide enough to toss a ball. If you are not interested a long walk, but want an outing with your dog, this park can't be beat.

Driving Directions

There are two approaches to Jacob's Island. If you are coming off I-90, exit at Van Buren Street and go south toward Broadway. Cross Broadway and find a parking spot (you can park near Missoula Chamber of Commerce on Front Street) and from there take the pedestrian bridge south toward the university and turn left on Jacob's Island, where you will see the park. If you are coming from Missoula, you can also access the park from the university side and the Kim Williams Nature Trail. In this case as you cross the pedestrian bridge, turn right to access the park.

Hiking Directions (see map on page 127)

It is really hard to get lost here—there is one path. If you follow the path to the end, there is an area with shallow water for dogs to play in. There have been reports of the fence not being completely dog proof, so if your dog is an escape artist, watch him carefully, since the escape route will bring him into a high traffic area.

Milo's Notes: I could have spent the day here. Balls, sticks, dogs, and people to pet me. My friend Petey the Corgi showed up—what a small dog (no pun intended) world.

Tank's Notes: I found a Frisbee abandoned next to a tree—I ate it. Tank-1, Frisbee-0.

Liz points out the dog sign to Tank at Pattee Canyon.

Pattee Canyon/Sam Braxton Trail
(4 Paws Up!)

Distance:	3.4 miles or longer
Time:	1–5 hours
Difficulty:	Easy to moderate

Overview

This area can be a bit overwhelming for a new visitor. There is such an abundance of trail and road options for hiking, mountain biking, and cross-country skiing, all of which are accessible from either the Crazy Canyon parking lot or the Sam Braxton trailhead (access from main Pattee Canyon). Even though this area gets high use from Missoulians, it is large enough to accommodate everyone, and within a few minutes you can get the solitude you want without ever feeling isolated (nice for solo hikers). Luckily, according to a Missoula native, if you are ever feeling lost, just head downhill and you will always end up back at Pattee Canyon Road, and from there, you should be able to find your vehicle. So go ahead, explore with your dog—there is so much ground to cover for both of you.

Many dog walkers, mountain bikers, and "Folf" (Frisbee Golf) players use this area, so make sure you and your dog are considerate hikers. When there is enough snow, the Missoula Nordic Ski Club grooms the trails for skate skiing. They ask that you leave your dog at home when using the groomed trails (but feel free to take them on un-groomed trails).

Driving Directions

In Missoula, take Southwest Higgins Avenue to Pattee Canyon Drive. Turn east and go about 3.9 miles to either the Crazy Canyon parking area (Pattee Canyon picnic area) or a little farther up, where the pavement ends at the Sam Braxton Trails parking area (the main trailhead).

Hiking Directions

If you are starting at the Sam Braxton trailhead, it is best to take a look at a map before venturing off. This trail is named after Sam Braxton, who was a well-known bicycle shop owner and outdoor enthusiast from Missoula. It's a nice, easy hike that leads you through cool forest trails under a canopy of mature ponderosa pines and western larch. Along the way look for remnants of an old homestead as well as a large assortment of birds that make their home in this mature forest.

Although there always seems to be enough water for a quick drink along the side of a trail or a stream for your dog, in the middle of summer you might want to carry a little extra for your buddy. The trail slowly climbs and loops around the Pattee Canyon Recreation Area for a nice 3.4-mile loop. The trail is signed, but it is intersected by old forest roads and other trails just enough to potentially be confusing.

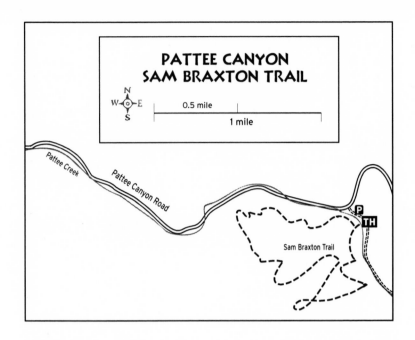

Just remember to head downhill if you are not sure of your location, and you will be fine!

Milo's Notes: There is a great picnic area here, if the timing were better, there might have been some good leftovers.

Tank's Notes: This is my territory—I love running as hard as possible with the mountain bikes, it tires me out.

Milo ready to run the Point Six Road.

Trail #42

Point Six Road

Distance: 4 miles round-trip
Time: 1 hour
Difficulty: Easy

Overview

Since this road is closed to traffic it is perfect for unadulterated dog running without distractions. It is in the forested hills, so it is very

133

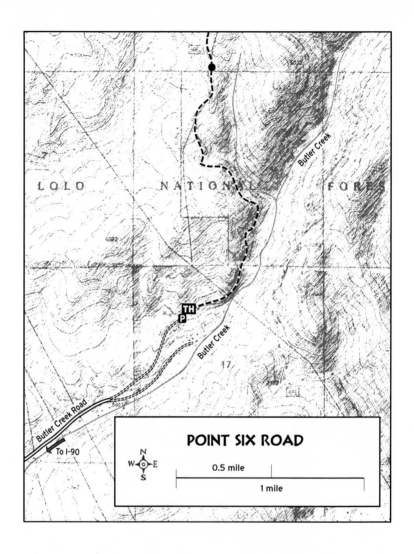

POINT SIX ROAD

0.5 mile

1 mile

quiet and shaded. Point Six Road is used for mountain biking as well as walking. It is a great place for visiting with a friend or daydreaming without having to think about the usual trail hazards that keep us watching where we take our next step. For getting out for pet (and person) exercise without having to travel far from Missoula, this is a great option. It's one of the few hikes that does not have a water source, so we like to bring a bowl for after-walking hydration.

Driving Directions

From Missoula, take I-90 west to Exit 99. Take the exit and go right (do not go under the highway bridge) and follow this road for 2 miles. The road name changes a few times from Keel Loop to Gooden Road. At the stop sign and another highway bridge to your left, turn right on Butler Creek Road. Drive this for 5 more miles. At the split in the road, veer left and continue straight on Six Point Road another half mile until it ends at the road gate.

Hiking Directions

The hiking directions are pretty easy for Point Six Road. Start at the gate and follow the road. It curves a couple times, lending views to tree-covered hillsides. If you choose to walk the road in its entirety, you will go about 5 miles and end up at the top of the hill with the communication towers and dishes. We like to go about 2 miles up (40 minutes) and turn around for the downhill. It is perfect for a furry family jog.

Milo's Notes: I love the chance to open it up on an expansive road.

Doc's Notes: There really aren't any danger factors for me on this one. I can just jiggle my way down the road feeling bad, bad, bad.

Sharing a drink after a stroll on Point Six Road.

Ravine Trail

Distance: 6 miles round-trip
Time: 2 hours
Difficulty: Easy

Overview

This is a great trail tucked away off the main Missoula grid. It is a north-facing, shaded canyon with some slight views. It makes for a great close-to-town hike or one off the highway if you are driving through and pining for some exercise. It is especially quiet and cool in the morning.

Driving Directions

From I-90, exit on Reserve Street (Exit 101) and turn north on Grant Creek Road. Drive about 4.4 miles past Snow Bowl Road. The trailhead is signed and is on your right on Grant Creek Road. There is parking at the trailhead.

Hiking Directions

Follow the trail from the parking lot, and it will gently climb in the lush and forested ravine. Within the first eighth mile there is a large puddle or a small pond that the dogs will sniff out to the left. This is the only water on the trail. The trail will begin a series of long switchbacks, providing treetop views of the surrounding environs. About 3 miles into the hike you come to a small clearing and vista of Missoula. This is a good turnaround point.

Milo's Notes: This was a cruiser. I especially loved cutting the corners of the switchbacks and hauling puppy butt down the trail.

Peety's Notes: I was a good trail guide, even with my little Cardigan Corgie legs. I showed these amateurs where the water hole was.

Doc, Uma, and Petey enjoy the shady canyon on the Ravine Trail.

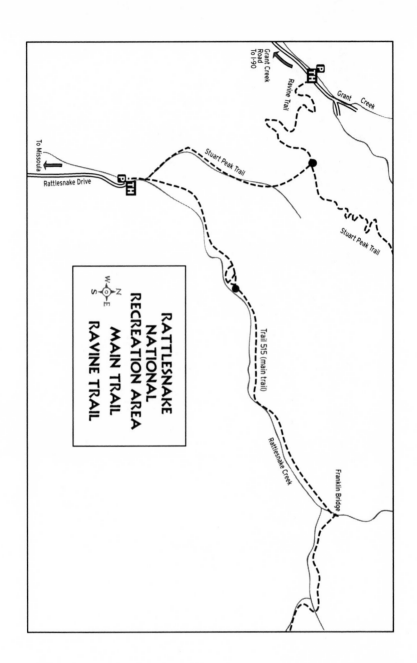

RATTLESNAKE
NATIONAL
RECREATION AREA
MAIN TRAIL
RAVINE TRAIL

Grant Creek Road To I-90

Ravine Trail

Grant Creek

To Missoula

Stuart Peak Trail

Rattlesnake Drive

Stuart Peak Trail

Trail 515 (main trail)

Rattlesnake Creek

Franklin Bridge

N
W — E
S

138

Risa and Holly walk Milo and Tank in the leash area of Rattlesnake Canyon.

Trail #44

Rattlesnake National Recreation Area

Distance: This is an out and back, with 73 miles of trails
available for use
Time: 1–8 hours (or an overnight)
Difficulty: Easy to strenuous

Overview

Only 4.5 miles outside Missoula, the Rattlesnake Recreation Area
offers a beautiful and serene option for dog walkers, runners, mountain
bike enthusiasts, and cross-country skiers. And, despite its forbidding
name, rattlesnakes are not common here. Although this is unquestion-
ably an incredible trail, dogs need to be on leash for the first 1.7 miles
for protection of water quality and to reduce wildlife conflicts. (When
we hiked it, only about 50% of the dog walkers were in compliance. Be

forewarned, you can be ticketed.) The trail is closed to dogs altogether from December 1 to February 28, in order to protect elk breeding. With that being said, this hike is still well worth it, whether you want to go for a short stroll or make a day of it. The trail (actually a road) follows Rattlesnake Creek through old growth ponderosa pine trees and shale rock outcroppings. There are several side trails, but watch the signs, many are either closed to dogs at certain times of the year, or never allow dogs. This is also very much a multiuse area, so make sure your dog is okay with mountain bikers, trail runners, and horses.

Driving Directions

Take the Van Buren Street exit off I-90 on the east end of Missoula and go 4.5 miles north on Rattlesnake Drive to the main parking area. The main trailhead has handicapped-access toilets, and there is another one 1.5 miles up the main corridor.

Hiking Directions (see map on page 138)

From the parking lot there are many choices of routes to take, but all of them start off along the main Rattlesnake Trail, which is the most dog friendly. Sawmill and Curry Gulch are closed for dogs, and Spring Gulch requires a leash for the first 1.3 miles (and is closed from December 1 through May 15).

As you follow the park-like road, Rattlesnake Creek is always in view, with large mature trees and shale outcroppings. Less than a half mile along the road, there is a trail to the left that heads up Spring Gulch to Stuart Peak, a steep 9.5-mile hike, but the first 3 miles are relatively flat. A little farther down the path, a trail cuts off from the road and brings hikers closer to the creek (great for dogs), if you are more interested in a short stroll for the day. For those interested in longer trips, the Rattlesnake Trail (515) continues for 9 miles along the creek and makes for a great out-and-back hike, allowing you and your dog to decide how far to go.

After the first few miles you will have a great, leash-free experience, with water for your dog and the beauty of the Rattlesnake for you.

Paw-Alternate: Another option in this area is to take the Woods Gulch trail, which is open to dogs off leash all year and for the entire length of the trail. To get to this trailhead, take a right turn instead of going left to the main trailhead and go about a half mile up Woods Gulch road. The road turns into a private road, and there are a couple of parking spots at the little trailhead. This is an extremely popular mountain bike trail, so be alert for bikes and make sure your dog is good at staying out of the way.

Milo's Notes: I just am not that comfortable on a leash, but it was worth spending some time on one to get into this hiking area.

Tank's Notes: I tried to eat the leash—Tank-1. Leash-0.

Liz with Milo and Tank along the Rattlesnake Canyon Trail.

Blue Mountain Recreation Area Maclay Flats Trail

Distance: 1–2 miles
Time: 30 minutes – 1 hour
Difficulty: Easy to moderate

Overview

The Blue Mountain Recreation Area just south of Missoula is one of the most popular areas for Missoulians to get out with their dogs for a quick afternoon stroll or a longer day hike. We chose to focus on Maclay Flats, because even though it is a leashed area, it does have great access for the Bitterroot River for swimming and playtime in the water. Blue Mountain has an extensive trail network that allows motorized use, mountain biking, and horses, as well as hikers. On most of the other Blue Mountain hikes there is little access to water, but on a cool day, or for a shorter hike with a post-hike dip in the river, this is a great Missoula area for dog lovers.

Driving Directions

From Reserve Street in Missoula, drive south on Highway 93 for 2 miles to Blue Mountain Road. Turn right at the light and travel about 1.5 miles on Blue Mountain Road. The parking area for Maclay Flats is on the right. There are several other hiking areas with trailheads along the road before and after the Maclay Flats parking area. Do not forget the leashes.

Hiking Directions

Maclay Flats is an easy 1.25- to 1.8-mile loop along a flat, wide trail that winds through meadows and park-like forests and follows the Bitterroot River. There are also interpretive signs that help identify the vegetative and animal life found throughout this area. The trail is used extensively by birders (hence dogs on leash), so bring along a pair of

Bitteroot River along Maclay Flats.

143

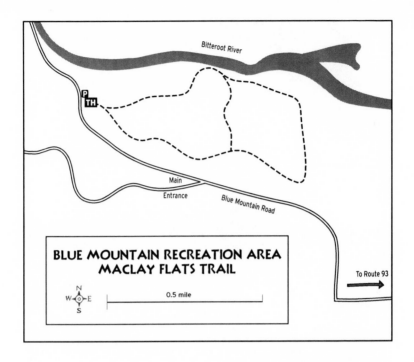

binoculars if you can. If you want to get to the river quickly, take a left as you start the trail. From there, it is less than a quarter of a mile to a nice beach, where you will find many dogs romping and swimming. Just make sure to re-leash your pet once you hit the trail again.

To explore the Blue Mountain Recreation Area further, there is a good trail map at the parking area—so pick a trail, and go for a hike!

Blue Mountain user designations (all allow dogs):

> Maclay Flats: Hikers only, dogs on leash

> Blue Mountain Nature Trail: Hikers only

> Blue Mountain National Recreation Trail:
Hikers and horses

> Motor Vehicle Trail and Forest Road 365:
Hikers, horses, mountain bikes, motorbikes, and ATVs

Milo, Doc, and Uma show they can be leashed at Maclay Flats.

Milo's Notes: I had to practice my leash etiquette here and try not to get tangled with Doc and Uma. It was way worth it for the swim.

Doc's Notes: You know, I really don't mind a leash so much. I must admit I prefer to roam, but a nice walk to a river with my friends is not a bad way to spend an hour or two.

View along Blodgett Canyon Trail.

Blodgett Canyon (4 Paws Up!)

Distance: 6 or more miles round-trip
Time: 3 hours
Difficulty: Easy

Overview

As you look down from the trail into Blodgett Creek, the water is so clear you just want to follow your dogs right into the stream and swim alongside them. Blodgett Canyon Trail follows Blodgett Creek almost the entire way and invites dogs and people in for cooling dips as you warm up from this slightly uphill and picturesque hike. This is the perfect hike for a warm day in the Bitteroot Valley or to escape the summer heat of Missoula.

Driving Directions

Traveling south from Missoula, turn right (west) onto Bowman Road (if you cross the Bitteroot River and go into Hamilton, you have gone too far). Go 0.6 miles on Bowman Road and turn left (south) onto Ricketts Road. Stay on Ricketts Road for 2 miles, taking a 90-degree turn to the west at a four-way intersection. Continue straight on what becomes Blodgett Camp Road for 4 miles to Blodgett Campground and Trailhead.

Hiking Directions

The trail starts right next to the Blodgett Canyon Campground. If your dog is warm from the ride, this is a great place for a quick dip and a drink before you start the hike. Blodgett Creek parallels the trail most of the way, but for the first 20 minutes, water is too far from the trail for dogs to access it.

After a few minutes and about 300 yards into this forested section of the trail, you will come to a memorial for Don Mackey, a smoke-jumper who grew up near Blodgett Canyon and was killed fighting the Storm King fire in Colorado.

147

The trail continues through the canyon, with magnificent views of the towering granite walls, deep pools for swimming, and the sound of flowing water as it cascades down through the creek. There are a few sections that cross boulder fields, and the trail becomes a bit challenging, so it is a good idea to watch your footing. At 3.1 miles a nice bridge crosses the creek, which we found was a good place to turn around. At 4.4 miles the trail goes by a waterfall and continues 12.5 miles to Blodgett Lake.

Milo's Notes: Make sure to stop at the flat rocks along the creek before the bridge; this was a great place for lunch and a swim.

Doc's Notes: This hike was perfect for me, not too long, not too steep, with lots of swimming time.

Uma's Notes: I didn't wander much here, those canyon walls kept me contained.

Milo follows Becky closely along the Blogett Trail.

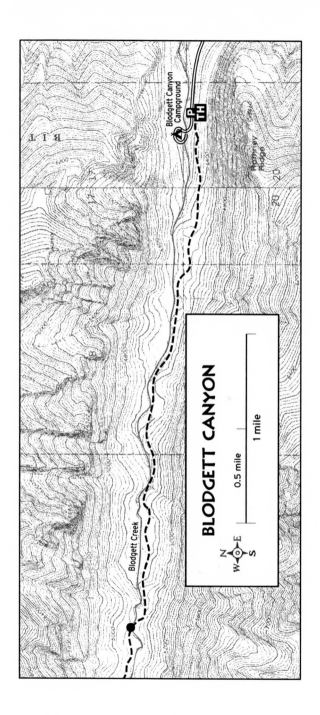

BLODGETT CANYON

N
W E
S

0.5 mile

1 mile

Blodgett Creek

Blodgett Canyon
Campground

Romney
Ridge

R 1 E

Flathead and Glacier Region

Milo runs along the Glacier Slough Trail.

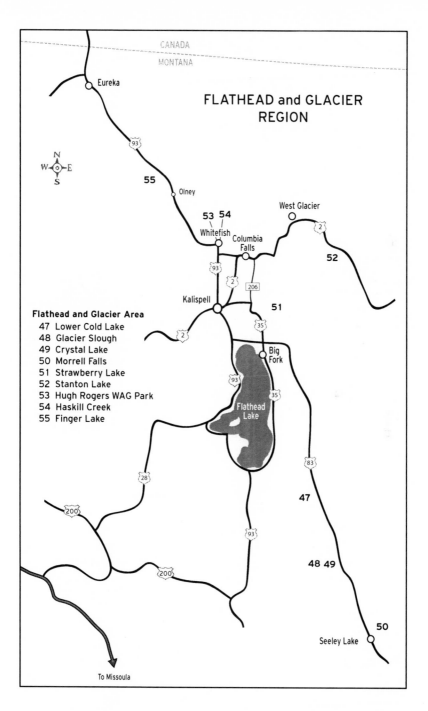

FLATHEAD and GLACIER REGION

CANADA
MONTANA

Eureka

93

55
Olney

53 54
Whitefish

West Glacier
2

Columbia
Falls

52

93

2

206

Kalispell

51

Flathead and Glacier Area
47 Lower Cold Lake
48 Glacier Slough
49 Crystal Lake
50 Morrell Falls
51 Strawberry Lake
52 Stanton Lake
53 Hugh Rogers WAG Park
54 Haskill Creek
55 Finger Lake

35

Big
Fork

93

35

Flathead
Lake

2

28

83

47

200

48 49

200

93

50

Seeley Lake

To Missoula

151

Lower Cold Lake

Distance: 5 miles round-trip
Time: 2.5 hours
Difficulty: Moderate

Overview

This hike in the Mission Mountains is a true wilderness experience. Through dense forest and across creeks, the hike lands you at a lovely alpine lake, complete with a distant waterfall. The creek crossings can be challenging during the early season while runoff continues, and they also can make for some muddy trail. This trail is narrow and rocky at times, requiring more awareness than some of our other walks, but it is very manageable and rewarding for you and your furry friends. It is bear country, so make noise, use bells, and do not forget the bear spray.

Driving Directions

From Kalispell take U.S. Highway 83 south for 44 miles to Cold Creek Road and turn right (west). Follow this for 3 miles, and take a slight right onto the North Fork of Cold Creek Road. Go another 2.3 miles and park at the trailhead.

Hiking Directions

Follow the trail up a steady climb through lush and dense forest. About 30 minutes into the hike, the trail will cross the creek. Depending on the time of the season and the flow, you might have to negotiate different approaches, but there are a handful of rock and log options. After crossing the creek, continue uphill. At times the trail runs through the creek bed itself. Before getting to the lake you will pass a swampy area on the right. There are plenty of boulders to have a rest, stare at the placid lake, then wild it up with a good dog swim or stick fetch.

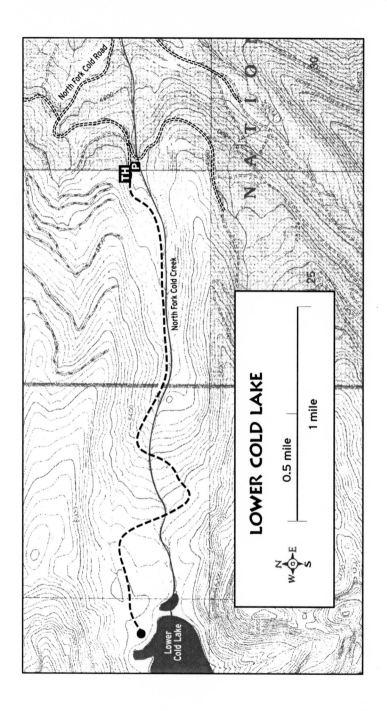

LOWER COLD LAKE

0.5 mile

1 mile

North Fork Cold Road

North Fork Cold Creek

Lower Cold Lake

TH
P

N
W   E
S

Milo's Notes: Ah, to be young and agile. I loved jumping across the creek, running up hill, then ending it with a cold swim.

Doc's Notes: This one was okay for me, since it wasn't too far, plus there weren't any scrambles. I got to warn the bears with my bell.

Becky crosses the river along Lower Cold Lake Trail.

Milo takes a swim at Glacier Slough.

Glacier Slough

Distance: 2.8 miles round-trip
Time: 1–2 hours
Difficulty: Easy

Overview

This is a short hike that makes you feel like you are deep in the wilderness. Walking only 1.4 miles, you come to a bend in Glacier Creek that is so wide that it looks more like a lake than a wide spot in the river. The slough provides clear reflections of the surrounding Mission Mountains. Sit for a while, throw sticks for the dog, and relax with a great view and the sounds of flowing water just around the bend.

Driving Directions

Take U.S. Highway 83 through the Swan Valley and turn onto the road to Lindbergh Lake between mile markers 34 and 35. Follow the road toward the Lindbergh Lake campground. At 3.5 miles there is a fork in the road (before the campground)—take the right toward Bunyan Lake. Check your odometer, since the trailhead is exactly 0.5 miles from the turn and a bit difficult to find. At 0.5 miles the road turns tightly to the left, and there is a turnoff on the right. Park here, and you will see a rustic sign for Glacier Slough Trail No. 481.

Hiking Directions

Even on a hot day, this hike stays cool for you and your dog as it weaves under the lush canopy of the Swan Valley. The hike starts out through a logged area with views of the Bob Marshall Wilderness and Mission Mountains. Although the mileage is short, there is varied terrain as the trail takes you through a natural depression (thus the name Glacier Slough), meadows, a mixed lodgepole and ponderosa pine forest, and lush areas covered with ferns. There are a few stream crossings, all with bridges or well-spaced rocks, so no worries about wet feet as your dog drinks from the clear flows. At the end of the trail, there are beautiful mountain views and a cool, slow-moving river, wide enough for a dog swim and some good stick chasing.

Milo's Notes: This trail had everything. A wide, slow-moving river to swim in, faster moving water to drink, and lots of sticks to chew—perfect.

Doc's Notes: This is a perfect wilderness hike for us elderly statesmen.

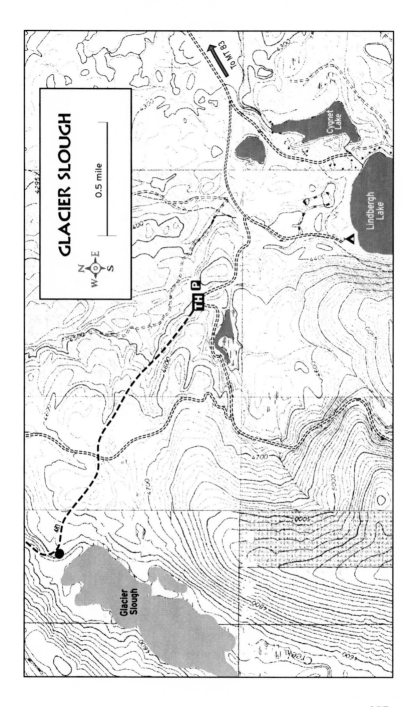

Milo at Crystal Lake.

Crystal Lake

Distance: 5.5 miles round-trip
Time: 3 hours
Difficulty: Moderate

Overview

The hike to Crystal Lake is best done in the morning while it is still cool. The good news is that the hike is downhill on the way there. The bad news is the climb out is not difficult, but it is steady and can be very warm in the afternoon. Since this is intended to be enjoyed with your favorite canine buddy, and the water holes along the way are few, morning is the best time for this destination. Did we mention that this is best walked in the morning?

Driving Directions

From Kalispell take U.S. Highway 83 south to Lindbergh Lake Road between mile markers 34 and 35 and turn right (west). Follow the road toward the Lindbergh Lake campground. At 3.5 miles there is a fork in the road (before the campground)—take the right toward Bunyan Lake. Follow the road for another 9 miles and park at the trailhead.

Hiking Directions

The trail takes you first through an open field with new growth and patches of bear grass. About a half mile into the hike, you will get to the top of the gulch. The next 2 miles of the hike are a steady downhill, with views of a tree-covered canyon and the Bob Marshall Wilderness. You will see some beautiful and quite large ponderosa pines along the way. The first spring and water relief is 45 minutes into the walk, just when your dog's tongue is dragging on the path.

The last half mile there are multiple creek and spring crossings, all doable, with well-placed rocks and logs. The trail will come to an unmarked junction, and you will want to take it to the right for the

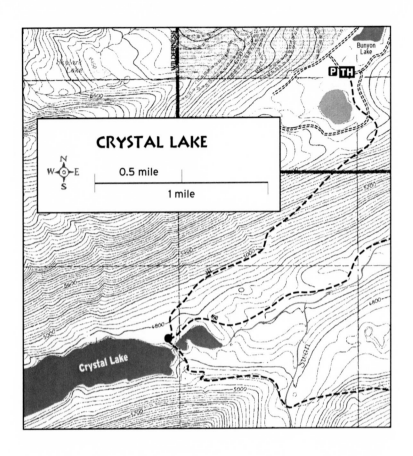

last steps to the lake. Plan on taking some time to enjoy the lake and getting the dogs (and you) nice and saturated before turning around and making the climb back.

Milo's Notes: It was confirmed on this hike that I have the longest tongue in western Montana.

Doc's Notes: I would sit this one out if I had to do it in the afternoon. Too warm with my fur coat.

160

Morrell Falls (4 Paws Up!)

Distance: 4.5 miles round-trip
Time: 2.5 hours
Difficulty: Easy

Overview

There is something rewarding about taking a hike in the woods that ends in stunning, cascading 90-foot waterfalls. This is an easy trail accessed just outside Seeley Lake in the Lolo National Forest that does just that. Plus there is enough shade and water to keep you comfortable until the final destination. If you go in the late season, you might even stumble across some huckleberry bushes, ripe for picking.

Driving Directions

From the town of Seeley Lake, drive a half mile north of town on U.S. Highway 83 and turn right (east) onto Morrell Creek Road. This becomes Forest Road 477 (Cottonwood Lakes Road). Go 1.1 miles. Turn left (north) on West Morrell Road 4353 and go about 6 miles. Turn east (right) on Pyramid Pass Road 4381 and go a quarter mile. Then turn left (north) on Morrell Falls Road 4364 and travel for 1 mile to the Morrell Falls trailhead and parking area.

Hiking Directions

Follow the trail sign and cross the creek onto the wide path. For the first 2 miles you will go through timber and groves of lodgepole pine and western larch. About 20 minutes before getting to the falls (depending on your and your pet's speed) you will come to Morrell Lake. This is a good drinking and plunging spot. From here you can hear the rush of the falls in the distance. Cross a bridge, and you have about 10 minutes following the path to the large stone falls. There are a handful of logs ideal for sitting to take in the view. If you are feeling energetic, about 30 yards before the falls, there is a turnoff path that climbs to the top and for a different perspective.

161

Morrell Falls.

Milo's Notes: I uncovered a new talent on this hike, I can sniff out huckleberries!! With this skill, I have a new nickname, "Huckleberry Hound." It works for me.

Doc's Notes: Perfect terrain and distance for a senior Golden. I really enjoyed a plunge in Morrell Lake before getting to the waterfalls.

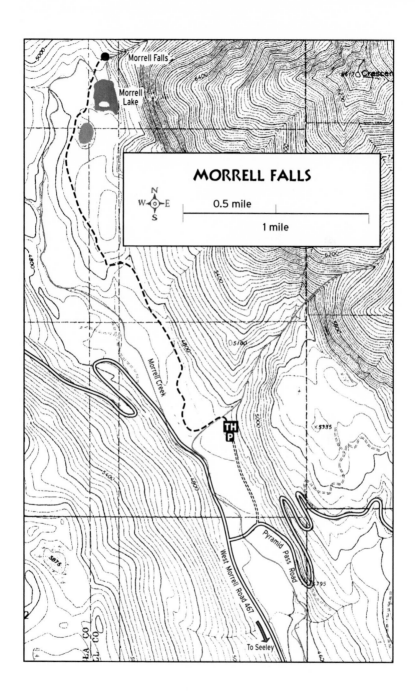

MORRELL FALLS

N W E S

0.5 mile

1 mile

Morrell Falls

Morrell Lake

Crescent

Morrell Creek

TH P

Pyramid Pass Road

West Morrell Road 467

To Seeley

Milo heads back after a dip in Strawberry Lake.

Strawberry Lake

Distance: 6 miles round-trip
Time: 3.5 hours
Difficulty: Moderate

Overview

With a bit of exertion, this switchbacking path takes you to some commanding views of the valley and drops you into a divine lake in the Jewel Basin. The path climbs steadily for the first 2.5 miles. It definitely keeps your heart going at a steady rate, but it is not strenu-

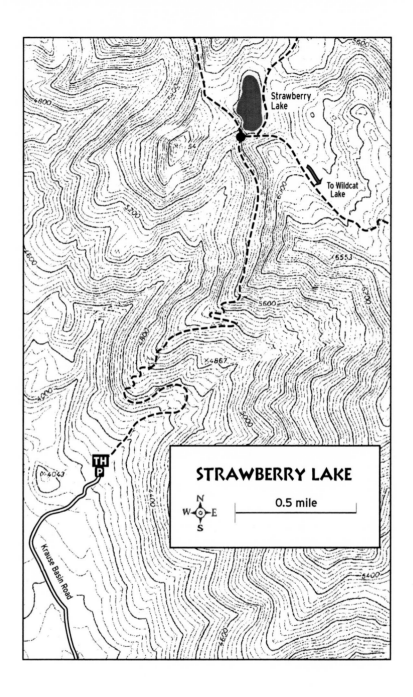

STRAWBERRY LAKE

0.5 mile

Strawberry Lake

To Wildcat Lake

Krause Basin Road

165

ous. There is water at the beginning of the hike and a small spring just before the lake. If you are worried about a hot and thirsty pooch, this hike might require an extra water bottle for the climb up, or tackling it in the morning might be best. There are also opportunities to catch your breath if you are hiking in late summer by picking at the loads of huckleberries along the way.

Driving Directions

From Columbia Falls, take U.S. 2 west 11 miles to MT-35 East. Turn left on MT-35 and drive 17 miles to MT-83 South and turn left. Take MT-83 South 3 miles to Echo Lake Road and turn left. Take this 2.2 miles to Foothill Road and turn right. Take Foothill Road 3.7 miles to Krause Basin Road. Follow Krause Basin Road and the signs to Strawberry Lake to the road's end, about 3.5 miles.

Hiking Directions

The trail starts by crossing the creek on a wide bridge. This is a good opportunity to get your pal (meaning your dog) nice and hydrated with a dip and drink. The next 2 miles are a steady climb up switchbacks without water. Follow the path up the switchbacks through the lush growth. At the top of the climb, you will have views of the valley, including surrounding lakes. The path turns the corner and drops slightly for the last half mile to the lake. The growth changes from forests to tall shrubs and flowers as you get to the lake. There are plenty of logs and sitting spots for a rest. If you desire a longer hike, you can pick up the trail to Wildcat Lake, another 2 miles.

Milo's Notes: My huckleberry hounding was in top form on this trail. I was glad Wendy and Becky brought baggies for collecting the berries.

Doc's Notes: This hike wore me out. I was glad to see rising fish at the lake and wish we could just drive to the lake next time.

Stanton Lake

Distance: 4 miles round-trip
Time: 1–2 hours
Difficulty: Easy with a few moderate pitches

Overview

Stanton Lake is located in the Great Bear Wilderness. It is close to, but not in, Glacier National Park. This trail allows you and your dog to get in a good hike (and possibly a swim) in the Glacier area, without crossing the national park boundary. It is a terrific stand-alone hike, but has the added appeal for those going into the park to get some of your pet's energy out before entering the park and having to contend with the many pet rules and regulations that go along with a national park.

Driving Directions

This hike is not well marked and a little hard to find. The trail is marked as Stanton Creek/Grant Ridge and can be accessed off Route 2 by taking the road to the right (north), directly east of Stanton Creek Lodge. Stanton Creek Lodge is located 16 miles east of West Glacier, Montana, on U.S. Highway 2 at mile marker 170.

Hiking Directions

There is no sign indicating that there is a trail to Stanton Lake, and if there are no other cars, the parking lot looks more like a clearing for logging trucks than a hiking area. After you park the car, head to the back of the parking area and toward the forest, where you will see a trail (it has a multiple use sign but no name). This is it.

Right away your heart will be pumping, as there is a steep climb for about the first 15 minutes. After the first incline the trail levels out and there is an overlook and view of the Great Northern Peak. It is a quick first mile to the beginning of the lake, however, there is no water between the trailhead and the lake. There is a trail junction at 0.9 miles

Milo takes a swim in Stanton Lake.

to Grant Pass, which as a side hike also has great views of the Great Northern.

Stanton Lake is the classic green blue of the Glacier area and has several small beaches along the shore for swimming and fishing. The end of the lake is a mile farther, with many more opportunities to swim or just take in the view of this incredible area. If you have time, the trail continues past the lake up to a meadow with nice mountain views.

Milo's Notes: Great swimming, and enough sticks to chase, so even my puppy energy was spent.

Doc's Notes: Perfect!

168

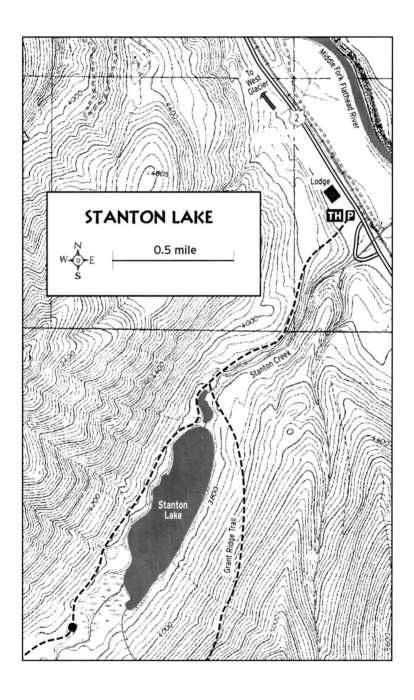

Hugh Rogers WAG Park

Distance: Less than a mile
Time: However long you want
Difficulty: Easy

Overview

Residents of Whitefish take their dogs and recreation with dogs seriously. After four years of hard work, the Hugh Rogers WAG (Whitefish Animal Group) Park was established on June 20, 2009. This 5-acre enclosed dog park features its own dog drinking fountain, great views, and best of all, a leash-free area for dogs and people to socialize right in town.

Driving Directions

Follow Route 93 north into Whitefish. This becomes Spokane Avenue. Take a right (east) on 2nd Street and follow 2nd for about 1 mile. The dog park will be on the right.

Hiking Directions

Enter through the double gate, and let your dog be the guide.

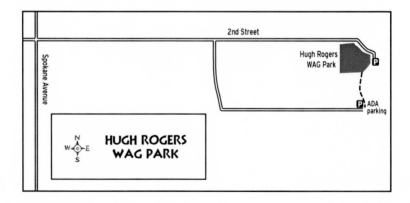

Milo gets a drink from the dog fountain at the dog park.

Milo's Notes: I always enjoy a good dog park. So many dogs to wrestle with!

Rio's Notes: Being the pint-sized Boston Terrier that I am, I like tussling it up with all the big dogs here.

Doc's Notes: The double fence entrance gate is a great idea for dogs like me eager to dash to the car.

Haskill Creek

Distance: 4 miles round-trip
Time: 1.5 hours
Difficulty: Easy

Overview

The town of Whitefish has access to a handful of logging roads that are closed to traffic, but open to walking, biking, and winter access. A few of these roads follow Haskill Creek, allowing a great opportunity for exercise and solitude close to town.

Driving Directions

From Whitefish, take Baker Avenue north of town (it turns into Wisconsin Avenue) and turn east on Edgewood Place. Follow this 2.5 miles (the road turns into East Edgewood Drive) to Haskill Basin Road. Turn north on Haskill Basin Road, and take this 1.9 miles to Haskill Creek Road. The street sign is hard to see, and the turn is a hairpin. Turn left on Haskill Creek Road. Take this about one-eighth of a mile to the first left turnout at a road with a metal barricade for traffic. Park at the turnout before the metal barracade.

Hiking Directions

The logging road goes through dark and lush western cedars about a quarter mile before reaching the creek. This is a good drinking spot before following the road up through the woods and basin. There are many options for walks and bike rides here. We like to set our watches and hike out and back. The creek is in the distance for the rest of the walk, which makes for a nice out and back to get a swim and drink before returning to the car. For aggressive doggie athletes, you can follow a logging road north about 5 miles, and it will end at the top of Haskill Creek Road, at another gate. This is great for mountain bikers, for they can ride the road back the 3 miles to their car at the start.

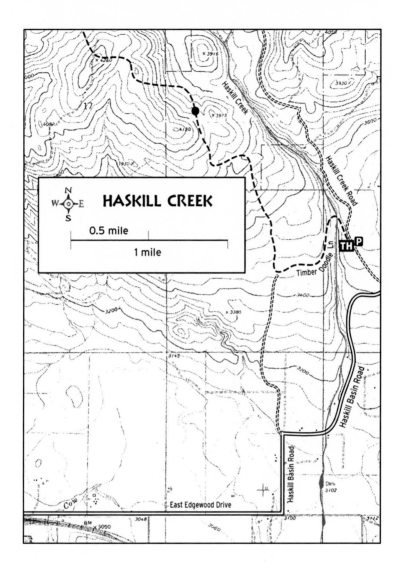

Milo's Notes: My huckleberry hounding was in top form on this trail. I could probably hire out like a truffle pig!

Furry Friend's Notes by "Rio" the Boston Terrier: This is the perfect hike for my little legs. Not too much gain and open road to walk by everyone's side.

Doc's Notes: Wide and open. This was my kind of hike.

Uma's notes: Grouse country…I could smell it immediately.

Milo thinks about a swim in the creek at Haskill Basin.

Milo checks out the rock cliffs at Finger Lake.

Finger Lake

Distance: 3 miles round-trip
Time: 1–2 hours
Difficulty: Easy with a few moderate pitches

Overview

Finger Lake is a local favorite in the Flathead Valley. It is a deep and clear lake surrounded by tall rock walls. This hike is great for a hot day when you and your dog need a swim. There are plenty lower beach areas for your dog to access the lake, and locals can be found jumping off the ledges for a plunge to cool off.

Driving Directions

From Whitefish, head north on route 93 toward Eureka. Take a left turn (west) on Radnor Road to Upper Stillwater Lake; the turn is 5.9 miles after the sign to Olney. After the turn, follow signs to Upper Stillwater Lake, following the main road. Do not take any side roads and proceed over the railroad tracks. After the tracks, take a sharp left up the hill at the Stillwater Lake sign. The sign for the trailhead will be on the right. If you get to the campground, you have gone too far.

Hiking Directions

The trail is well marked at the parking area. The first part is a wide four-wheel-drive road, but it soon narrows to a single track. It is a relatively easy hike with a few steep pitches and gets you to the lake in very little time. On the way back, make sure to follow the trail to the left when it forks, to get back to the parking area. The scenery during the hike is forest, so no large vistas, but the lake at the end makes it worth it.

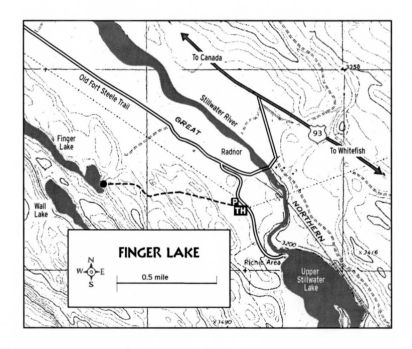

Milo cools off at Finger Lake.

Milo's Notes: There were several other groups of people and dogs enjoying the day when we were there—those crazy people, jumping off the cliff. I am glad Wendy didn't make me join them.

Doc's Notes: It was a little steep getting down to the lake. I would have been content just watching all the action.

Trails Not So Great for Dogs

One of the many attractive attributes of western Montana is that most towns have a variety of easily accessible and appealing hikes to offer. As hikers, we too love these options. There are a handful of popular trails where many hikers bring their dogs along, however, we would recommend steering away from these hikes. Our recommendation to avoid the following hikes with your pet is due to a variety of elements such as full sun exposure, tremendous use and popularity of the trail, or lack of water.

Bozeman Area

Leverich Canyon: There is heavy mountain bike traffic.

The M Trail: The MSU "M" trail is easy to access and does have some shade, however, the lack of water and crowds makes it not the best choice when there are so many others in the area.

Sypes Canyon: There is not any water and a great deal of mountain biking traffic.

Butte, Helena Region

Delmoe Lake area: There is heavy motorized use.

Mount Helena: This is leash only.

Missoula Region

Lubrecht Experimental Forest: Trails are not well maintained, no water, and exposed areas.

The M Trail: The town landmark is certainly fun to climb, but there is no water or shade, and it requires leashes.

Snow Bowl Ski Area: Restricted use.

Whitefish/Glacier

All trails in Glacier National Park. There is a dogs-only-in-parking-lots-and-campgrounds policy.

Yellowstone Park Area

All trails in Yellowstone National Park. There is a dogs-only-in-parking-lots-and-campgrounds policy.

Appendix: Pet References

The following pages list pet-friendly hotels, stores, and local veterinarians. Establishments can come and go in our towns, so be sure to call to confirm policies.

Another tool for finding pet-friendly accommodations is petswelcome.com. It is a robust search site to help with traveling needs with animals.

BIG SKY/GALLATIN CANYON

Pet-Friendly Lodging

320 Guest Ranch
($10 per pet, per night. Pets must be kept leashed and under control at all times.)
Gallatin Canyon, Big Sky
(406) 995-4283
www.320ranch.com

Bucks T4 Lodge
(two dogs of any size for $10/night)
46625 Gallatin Road, Big Sky
(406) 995-4111
www.buckst4.com

Rainbow Ranch Lodge
($10 per night, dogs receive their own bed, water bowl, and treats. Advance notice is requested.)
42950 Gallatin Road, Big Sky
(406) 995-4132
www.rainbowranchbigsky.com

Veterinarians
See Bozeman for Veterinarians.

BIG TIMBER/LIVINGSTON

Pet Boarding

Absaroka Pet Ranch, Inc.
(406) 223-7822

Pet-Friendly Lodging

The Best Western Yellowstone Inn
1515 West Park Street, Livingston
(406) 222-6110

The Murray Hotel
201 West Park Street, Livingston
(406) 222-1350, www.murrayhotel.com

Quality Inn
111 Rogers Lane, Livingston
(877)424-6423

Veterinarians

All Creatures Veterinary Services
22 Highway 10 E., Big Timber
(406) 932-4324

Colmey Veterinary Hospital
5288 U.S. Highway 89 S, Livingston
(406) 222-1700

Livingston Veterinary Hospital
1104 E Park Street, Livingston
(406) 222-2011

BOZEMAN

Pet Boarding

Animal House Pet Lodging
(406) 599-0902

BarkCity Doggy Day Care
(406) 587-6252

Doggie Daycare & Motel (Gallatin
Gateway)
(406) 763-5585

Kennels West Dog Boarding
(406) 587-7446

Montana Veterinary Hospital
(406) 586-2019

Tail Waggin Ranch
(406) 388-7387

Valley View Veterinary Boarding
(406) 586-9094

West Veterinary Hospital
(406) 586-4919

Pet-Friendly Lodging

The Best Western Grantree Inn
1325 North 7th Avenue, Bozeman
(406) 587-5261

The Holiday Inn
5 East Baxter Lane, Bozeman
(406) 587-4561

La Quinta Inn and Suites
620 Nikles Drive, Bozeman
(406) 585-9300

Western Heritage Inn of Bozeman
1200 East Main Street, Bozeman
(406) 586-8534

Pet Stores

Barkenhowell's
East Main Street, Bozeman
(406) 586-6160
www.barkenhowells.com

Dee-O-Gee
West Main Street, Bozeman
(406) 551-2364
www.dee-o-gee.com

PetSmart Bozeman
2997 Max Avenue, Bozeman
(406) 522-1515

Veterinarians

Banfield Pet Hospital, at PetSmart
2997 Max Avenue, Bozeman
(406) 586-0334

Cottonwood Veterinary Hospital
450 Cottonwood Road, Bozeman
(406) 582-0555
www.cottonwoodvet.net

BUTTE REGION

Pet Boarding

Tadroh Kennel
1461 Longfellow Street, Butte
(406) 494-3689

Pet-Friendly Lodging

Best Western Plus Butte Plaza Inn
2900 Harrison Ave., Butte
(406) 494-3500

Comfort Inn Butte
2777 Harrison Ave., Butte
(406) 494-8850

Copper King Mansion
219 W. Granite St., Butte
(406) 782-7580

Rocker Inn
122001 W. Browns Gulch Rd., Butte
(406) 723-5464

Pet Stores

Quality Supply
3939 Harrison Ave., Butte
(406) 494-4044

Veterinarians

Amherst Animal Hospital
2330 Amherst, Butte
(406) 494-4044
www.amherstanimalhosp.com

Butte Veterinary Services
6000 Harrison Ave., Butte
(406) 494-3635

HELENA REGION

Pet-Friendly Lodging

Appleton Inn and Bed & Breakfast
1999 Euclid Ave., Helena
(406) 443-7330

Barrister Bed and Breakfast
416 N. Ewing St., Helena
(406) 443-7330

Best Western Helena Great Northern Hotel
835 Great Northern Blvd., Helena
(406) 457-5500

Shilo Inn & Suites
202 Prospect Ave., Helena
(406) 442-0320

Pet Stores

Petco
3215 Dredge Drive, Helena
(406) 449-7461

Pet Town
1401 11th Ave., Helena
(406) 443-7669

Veterinarians

Alpine Medical Clinic
1801 Cedar, Helena
(406) 449-7155
www.alpineanimalclinic.com

Companion Animal Hospital
4880 N. Montana Ave., Helena
(406) 449-4455
www.companionanimalhospital.com

Helena Veterinary Services
2830 N. Montana Ave., Helena
(406) 442-6450
www.helenavets.com

Montana Veterinary Specialists
1660 Euclid Ave., Helena
(406) 449-3539
www.montanavetspecialists.com

MISSOULA REGION

Pet-Friendly Lodging

Best Western Grant Creek Inn
(a one-time $10 fee—no weight limit or restriction on the number of pets allowed per room)
5280 Grant Creek Road, Missoula
(406) 543-0700
(877) 411-3436

Days Inn Missoula Airport
(two dogs of any size $5/night per pet)
8600 Truck Stop Road, Missoula
(406) 721-9776
www.Daysinn.com

Doubletree Hotel Missoula/Edgewater
(two dogs of any size for $20, plus $10 for each pet)
100 Madison Street, Missoula
(406) 728-3100
www.Doubletree.com

La Quinta Inn
(two dogs under 10 lbs. for $10/night each)
5059 North Reserve Street, Missoula
(406) 549-9000
(877) 411-3436
www.Laquinta.com

Red Lion Inn Missoula
(All Red Lion hotels are now pet-friendly. The hotel allows up to two pets, 30 lbs. or less, per room. Pets stay free if owners are members of the Red Lion R&R.)
700 West Broadway, Missoula
(406) 728-3300
www.Red-Lion-Inn-Missoula.com

Super 8 Missoula
(two dogs of any size $5/night per pet)
3901 South Brooks Street, Missoula
(406) 251-2255
(877) 411-3436

Pet Stores

Go Fetch
627 Woody Street, Missoula
(406) 728-2275

Quick Paws Hiking Company
1720 S 3rd Street West, Missoula
(406) 721-1943

Veterinarians

Alpine Veterinary Services
500 S 5th St. W, Missoula
(406) 728-4605

Eastgate Veterinary Clinic
1001 E Broadway St. # 7, Missoula
(406) 728-0095

Emergency Animal Clinic
1914 S Reserve St., Missoula
(406) 829-9300

Four Paws Veterinary Clinic
2625 Connery Way, Missoula
(406) 542-3838

RED LODGE

Pet-Friendly Lodging

Comfort Inn
612 N. Broadway, Red Lodge
(406) 446-4469
www.comfortinn.com/hotel-red_lodge-
montana-MT010

Lupine Inn
702 S. Hauser, Red Lodge
(888) 567-1321
www.lupineinn.com
Yodeler Motel
601 S. Broadway, Red Lodge
(866) 446-1435
www.yodlermotel.com

Veterinarians

Grizzly Peak Animal Hospital
7165 U.S. Highway 212, Red Lodge
(406) 446-1778

Red Lodge Veterinary Clinic
178 Highway 78, Red Lodge
(406) 446-2815

WHITEFISH/GLACIER/KALISPELL

Pet Boarding

A Pet Boarding Retreat (PBR Kennels)
1836 Trumble Creek Road, Kalispell
(406) 257-4363
(406) 270-9821
www.petboardingretreatkennels.com

Lucky Dog Daycare
Kalispell
(406) 257-5825

Three Dog Ranch (Whitefish)
5395 US Highway 93 S, Whitefish
(406) 862-3913
www.threedogranchmontana.com

Triple R Kennels
Columbia Falls
(406) 892-3695
(406) 270-7736
www.triplerkennels.com

Pet-Friendly Lodging

Bay Point on the Lake
(pets allowed in five pet rooms)
300 Bay Point Drive, Whitefish
(406) 862-2331
(800) 327-2108
www.baypoint.org

Bar W Guest Ranch
(call for information)
2875 U.S. Highway 93 West, Whitefish
(406) 863-9099
(866) 828-2900
www.thebarw.com

Best Western Rocky Mountain Lodge
(two dogs of any size for $15/night for
one pet; $20/night for two)
6510 Highway 93 South, Whitefish
(406) 862-2569
(877) 411-3436
www.Bestwestern.com

Big Mountain Lodge/Holiday Inn Express
(two dogs of any size for $15/night, non-smoking)
6390 South U.S. 93, Whitefish
(406) 862-4020
(877) 411-3436

Downtowner Inn
(two dogs of any size for $20/stay per pet)
224 Spokane Avenue, Whitefish
(406) 862-2535
(877) 411-3436
www.downtownermotel.cc

The Hidden Moose Lodge
(two dogs of any size for a fee of $10/night each)
1735 E Lakeshore Dr., Whitefish
(406) 862-6516
www.bedandbreakfast.com

The Outlaw Hotel
(two dogs under 50 lbs. in each guest room for a one-time fee of $15 each)
1701 Highway 93 S, Kalispell, MT
(406) 755-6100
(877) 411-3436
www.outlawhotel.com

Red Lion Hotel Kalispell
(All Red Lion hotels are now pet-friendly. The hotel allows up to two pets, 30 lbs. or less, per room. Pets stay free if owners are members of the Red Lion R&R.)
North 20 Main, Kalispell
(406) 751-5050
(877) 411-3436
www.rdln.com

Super 8 Whitefish
(additional fee of $10 per pet per night)
800 Spokane Avenue, Whitefish
(406) 862-8255
(877) 411-3436
www.super8.com

Travelodge Kalispell
($10/night each—no weight limits or other restrictions at this hotel)
350 North Main Street, Kalispell
(406) 755-6123

(877) 411-3436
www. travelodge.com

Veterinarians

All Creatures Veterinary Clinic
524 W Reserve Dr., Kalispell
(406) 756-6513

Big Sky Animal Clinic
15 18th St. E, Kalispell
(406) 755-2010
bigskyanimalclinic.com

Glacier Animal Hospital
511 2nd Ave. West, Columbia Falls
(406) 892-4319

Whitefish Animal Hospital
245 W. 2nd Street, Whitefish
(406) 862-3178

YELLOWSTONE PARK REGION

Pet Boarding

See Bozeman for pet boarding

Pet-Friendly Lodging

Best Western Desert Inn
(one dog of any size)
133 Canyon, West Yellowstone
(406) 646-7376
(877) 411-3436
www.bestwesternmontana.com

Clubhouse Inn
(two dogs up to 25 lbs, smoke free)
105 South Electric St., West Yellowstone
(406) 646-4892
(877) 411-3436
www.yellowstoneclubhouseinn.com

Grey Wolf Inn and Suites
(must stay in smoking rooms)
250 S Canyon St., West Yellowstone
(406) 646-0000
(877) 411-3436
www.visityellowstonepark.com

Kelly Inn
(only on ground floor, two dogs of any
size allowed)
104 South Canyon, West Yellowstone
(406) 646-4544
(877) 411-3436
www.yellowstonekellyinn.com

Yellowstone Lodge
(two dogs of any size)
251 S Electric Ave., West Yellowstone
(406) 646-0020
(877) 411-3436
www.yellowstonelodge.com

Pets are allowed in Yellowstone National
Park Campground but with very strict
regulations—you might want to consider
boarding your dog when visiting the
park.

There are no boarding facilities in West
Yellowstone, but many can be found in
the surrounding area.

Veterinarians

High West Veterinary Services
201 S Canyon St., West Yellowstone
(406) 646-4410

Index

CPSIA information can be obtained at www.ICGtesting.com
Printed in the USA
268436BV00001B/4/P